42 Etudes For The Violin

3420

EDITION WHITE-SMITH No. 114

RODOLPHE KREUTZER
1766–1831

42

STUDIES or CAPRICES
FOR THE
VIOLIN

Edited by EMIL KROSS

English Text by AMBROSE DAVENPORT

Copyright, 1893, by White-Smith Music Publishing Co.

WHITE-SMITH MUSIC PUBLISHING CO.
BOSTON   NEW YORK   CHICAGO

Emil Kross' arrangement of Kreutzer's 42 Etudes betokens intimate knowledge, industry and talent, and is to be recommended to all teachers and students as the best.

BERLIN, May 1885.
PROF. H. DE AHNA.

The arrangement of Kreutzer's Studies by Emil Kross has been accomplished with endless care and fidelity. They will not only inspire enthusiasm in the teacher, but a thorough understanding of the markings and of their various inculcations and demands will prove of inestimable value when put in practice.

BERLIN, May 1885.
JOSEPH JOACHIM.

DEAR SIR:

Your work in the Kreutzer 42 Etudes, I have to-day thoroughly examined with great interest. Through their accurate and conformable markings they supply a real necessity. Should you find a publisher for your work, and I hope you will, I shall then have the pleasure of introducing the edition into my class and of recommending it above all others.

HUGO HEERMANN.

WEIMAR, October 15, 1884.

VERY DEAR SIR:

At last it is possible for me to accede to your wish by forwarding you my opinion as regards your markings of the Kreutzer Etudes. Master Liszt sent them to me recently. The independence of the fingers of the left hand, through your markings, it appears to me, will receive special and complete development. The labor which you have bestowed upon this work evinces wonderful industry and profound thought. The result cannot fail to be a success.

With friendly greeting.

Accept my highest regards,
AUG. KOMPEL.

Kreutzer's Etudes for the Violin as arranged by Emil Kross, I can recommend. They contain manifold bowings which do not appear in the earlier editions, and for which, when we consider the present art of playing, there was no necessity. In reference to the 10th Etude in G major, I would say that in the same form in which it is registered as 10b it will be found in the right place. The study of this 2d Etude, on account of the fingerings is particularly useful. In general great care has been exercised in the indications of the fingering, so, also with the text, thus greatly facilitating study. The succession of the Etudes, which have been arranged in order according to their difficulty—although somewhat new—is consistent throughout and to be recommended. Attested.

HAMBURG, March 1885.

JEAN JOSEPH BOTT,
Court Chapel Master to the King.

Die von Herrn Emil Kross bearbeiteten 42 Kreutzer's Etuden beweisen viel Sachkenntniss, Fleiss und Talent und sind Lehrenden and Lernenden bestens zu empfehlen.

BERLIN, Mai 1885.
PROF. H. DE AHNA.

Die Bearbeitung der Kreutzer'schen Uebungen durch H Kross ist mit unendlicher liebevoller Sorgfalt ausgefuhrt. Si sehr anregend fur den Lehrer, und die Befolgung der Bezeichnung wird von ausserordentlichem Nutzen sein konnen, wenn der B ffende die Fulle des Gebotenen und Verlangten mit Urthe benutzen versteht.

BERLIN, Mai 1885.
JOSEPH JOACHIM.

GEEHRTESTER HERR!

Ihre Arbeit uber die Kreutzer'schen 42 Etuden habe ich grossem Interesse heute durchgesehen, und fullen Sie durch genaue und sachgemasse Bezeichnung eine wahre Lucke aus. ten Sie einen Verleger fur Ihre Arbeit finden, was ich hoffe werde ich mit Vergnugen bereit sein, die Ausgabe in meine Cl einzufuhren und sie uberall empfehlen.

HUGO HEERMANN.

WEIMAR, am 10. Oktober 1884.

Sehr geehrter Herr!

Endlich ist es mir moglich, Ihrem Wunsche nachzukomn mich uber Ihre Bezeichnung der Kreutzer'schen Violin-Etuden aussern. Meister Liszt ubersandte sie mir unlangst. Die U hangigkeit der Finger der linken Hand scheint mir durch) Bezeichnung ganz besonders gepflegt werden zu sollen. D Bezeichnung ist eine Arbeit von bewunderungswurdigem Fleiss Nachdenken. Die Erfolge werden nicht ausbleiben.

Mit freundlichem Gruss.

Ihr hochachtungswoll ergebener
AUG. KOMPEL.

Die Bearbeitung der Kreutzer'schen Violin-Etuden du Herrn Emil Kross kann ich empfehlen. Dieselbe enthalt v Stricharten, welche in den fruhern Ausgaben nicht vorhanden fur die jetzige Spielart durchaus, nothwendig sind. In Bezug die 10te Etude in g dur erwahne ich, dass dieselbe in der Weise, sie im Register als 10 b angegeben ist, ihren richtigen Platz fin Das Studium dieser 2tem Etude ist wegen ihres Fingersa entschieden Nutzen bringend.—Ueberhaupt ist grosse Sorgfa die Bezeichnung des Fingersatzes gelegt, sowie auch der Text Studium bedeutend erleichtert. Die Reihenfolge der Etuden, wel nach ihrer Schwierigkeit geordnet wurde, ist—obgleich etwas Ne —doch als durchaus zweckmassig zu empfehlen. Dies attestirt.

HAMBURG, den 16, Marz 1885.

JEAN JOSEPH BOTT
Konigl. Hofcapellmeister.

PREFACE.

Although there are several editions of Rudolph Kreutzer's celebrated Etudes in existence, I have seen the necessity of another which I hope, through my markings, will enable the student to achieve quicker results and at the same time build up a solid and correct technic. These Etudes of R. Kreutzer, in connection with a careful study of the scales, are the daily bread of every violinist who desires to acquire complete mastery of the bow and fingerboard. The accomplished violinist often takes occasion to review what he has previously studied, and to go over anew the matter that has enabled him to acquire his technic, and especially so as regards many of the Kreutzer Etudes, which through their artistic beauty have served to form his musical taste and to imbue him with a love for classical music.—When one knows the means by which the way may be shortened, he should feel it a duty to impart that knowledge to others. I desire to explicitly remark that this edition will reveal to many talented, *independent violinists* who are not wholly satisfied with their own playing, how, through attention, accuracy, consequently energy, the way may be made clear by which they can perfect their own abilities. With other editions they will very often be obliged, without the assistance of a competent teacher, to guess at many things which in this edition will be found carefully indicated. Only a small proportion of players have the favorable opportunity to study with a teacher of great superiority, and thereby arrive at a high degree of proficiency; and many evincing talent and assiduity, after laying a *good foundation* with the help of a teacher, from which a still higher degree of development may be evolved, find in their limited environment, but a poor chance perhaps, for practical observation, or of gaining advice, or of experiencing the stimulating effect of often hearing an acknowledged master, or of enjoying the advantages of consultation with a capable and solid violin teacher. To the diligent I doubt not this edition will be welcome. It is in the sense of the preceding that I wish to have this work regarded. In certain suitable numbers I have considered one condition—that of the *lying-idle, unoccupied fingers*, which, in no edition of Kreutzer have I yet found. One more quickly gains thereby great strength and independence of the fingers; further, the very considerable advantage of a fine finger-feeling, and consequently the obtaining more quickly a purer, surer intonation and a brilliant clearness in the figures and passages. Moreover one acquires almost intuitively the art of double-stop playing. In other Violin-schools this principle is already in use, although only through a figure-marking of the idle or unemployed fingers, and not as is the case in the present edition by silently fingering the notes [notation] which also indicate the passing over of the fingers. A second principle in this edition consists in using the 2d, 4th and 6th Positions in conjunction with the 1st, 3d, 5th and 7th. In other editions of Kreutzer's Etudes, one mostly finds only the odd positions 1, 3, 5, and 7, presumably for the reason that they are found more convenient and natural; and in going towards the bridge, the crest of the hand at the edge, on the projection of the neck offers the advantage of firmness, comfort and surely in playing. Only in cases of absolute necessity, where it is positively required, are the uneven positions 2, 4, and 6, indicated.

VORWORT.

Obgleich einige Ausgaben von Rudolph Kreutzer's beruhmten Violin-Etuden existiren, habe ich mich zu einer solchen veranlasst gesehen, weil ich hoffe, dass der Studirende durch meine Bezeichnung schneller zum Ziele gelangt, sich eine solide und correcte Technik anzueignen. — R. Kreutzer's Violin-Etuden sind in Verbindung mit dem sorgfaltigen Scalen-Studium das tagliche Brod jedes Violinisten, der seiner Herrschaft uber Bogen und Griffbrett sicher bleiben will. Auch der fertige Geiger kommt oft darauf zuruck und durchlauft gern den Weg von Neuem, auf welchem er seine Technik erlangt hat, zumal auch viele von Kreutzer's Etuden seinen Geschmack durch ihre Kunstschonheit gebildet und seine Vorliebe fur classische Musik angeregt werden haben.—Weiss man nun Mittel, diesen Weg abzukurzen, so fuhlt man sich verpflichtet, auch Andere auf dieselben aufmerksam zu machen. Ausdrucklich mochte ich noch bemerken, dass diese Ausgabe manchem begabten *alleinstehenden Geiger*, welcher mit seinem Spiele unzufrieden ist, bei nothiger Aufmerksamkeit, Genauigkeit, Consequenz und Energie sicher den Weg bahnen wird, dasselbe bald zu veredeln. Aus andern Ausgaben wird er sehr Vieles ohne einen gediegenen Lehrer zu errathen gezwungen sein, was er in dieser Ausgabe genau verzeichnet findet. Nur einer verhaltnissmassig kleinen Anzahl von Geigern hat es die Gunst der Verhaltnisse gestattet, bei einem bedeutenden Lehrer Studien zu machen, und so Mancher, welcher das Talent und die Strebsamkeit besitzt, nach einer bei einem Lehrer erlangten *guten Grundlage* auf eine hohere Stufe zu gelangen, sieht sich bei seinem in einer kleinen Stadt angewiesenen Wirkungskreise leider rathlos um, da ihm sowohl die Anregungen durch das oftere Horen der Meister als auch die Gelegenheiten zum Consultiren tuchtiger gediegener Violinlehrer fehlen. Diesen Strebsamen wird diese Ausgabe eine sehr willkommene sein. In vorstehendem Sinne wunsche ich diese Bearbeitung betrachtet zu sehen.—In den dazu geeigneten Nummern habe ich auch das *Liegen-Lassen unbeschaftigter Finger* im Auge gehabt, was ich noch in keiner Kreutzer-Ausgabe bezeichnet gefunden habe. Man gelangt dadurch schneller zu grosserer Kraftigung und Unabhangigkeit der Finger, ferner zu dem so wichtigen Vortheil einer feineren Ausbildung des Tastgefuhls und demnach schneller zu einer reinen sichern Intonation und einer brillanten Klarheit in den Figuren und Passagen. Ferner lernt man durch die stumm zu greifenden Noten schon bei einfachen Passagen unbewusst in Doppelgriffen spielen. In einer Violinschule ist dieses Princip ebenfalls schon angewandt' allerdings nur durch bezifferte liegenbleibende Finger und nicht auch wie es bei dieser Ausgabe der Fall durch stumm zu greifende Noten [notation] welche auch das Uebersetzen der Finger markiren. Ein zweites in dieser Ausgabe durchgefuhrtes Princip besteht in haufigerer Anwendung der 2, 4, und 6, Lage neben der ersten, dritten, funften und siebenten. In andern Ausgaben der Kreutzer'schen Etuden sind hauptsachlich die ungeraden Lagen 1, 3, 5, und 7, angewendet und zwar aus dem Grunde, weil diese Lagen die geigenmassigsten und naturlichsten sind, in denen es sich wegen der Stutze der Hand am Sattel und am Vorsprung des Halses an den Zargen am bequemsten und sichersten spielt. Nur zur grossten Noth, und wenn es durchaus sein muss, fin-

IV

However, this preference for the odd positions is not always the most artistic to employ, considered from a technical standpoint, or even the most advantageous in musical performance, especially in legato-passages, in which the long change of position being heard much more perceptibly than in the shorter, is often very strongly apparent. For this reason it is frequently enjoined in this edition to make the change of position at the half-tone, for by a shorter skip of the hand a greater smoothness of playing may be obtained. The change of position at the half-tone may be made by *any one* of the *four fingers*, and we can by this means move equally well upward or downward or pass occasionally, at an opportune moment, into another position and return. (See Ex.)

det man die geraden Positionen 2, 4, und 6, Lage verzeichnet. J doch ist diese Bevorzugung der ungeraden Positionen nicht au immer dem musikalischen Vortrage zutraglich, was besonders b Legato-Passagen, in welchen der Lagenwechsel selbstverständli mehr als in gestossenen zu horen ist, oft sehr merkbar hervortri Aus diesem Grunde ist in dieser Ausgabe oft darauf Rucksic genommen worden, dass der Lagenwechsel *beim halben Ton* eintri um durch einen kurzeren Sprung der Hand eine grossere Glatte d Spiels zu erzielen. Den Lagenwechsel auf dem halben Ton kar *jeder der vier Finger* ubernehmen, und kann man in dieser Wei sowohl herauf als herabsteigend bei passenden Gelegenheiten eine andere Lage einkehren z. B

As authority for the last remark I would cite the famous virtuoso Charles de Beriot, who has advanced the same in the 2d part of his great and acknowledged superior Violinschool. As to what de Beriot has done besides his solo-work and as teacher considered, the many famous masters who have gone from his School—Vieuxtemps, Prume, Leonard and others bear testimony. L. Spohr also held this opinion, and in his great Violinschool, regarding the production of the tone with the 1st and 4th fingers, he takes occasion to say concerning his E major Study in the 3d position: "When a tone is to be played with the next one in succession, both together in one bowstroke, there should be only a half-tone between, because, when a whole tone exists, through the movement of the finger *a disagreeable sound* will be heard."

Spohr in editing his school studies as well as other violin compositions, often omitted to mention that the sliding of the fingers which is so perceptible in slurred passages when slow notes follow each other, is always noticeable at a change of position as soon as the change is effected on a whole tone; not only in the downward drawing but also in the upward gliding of each of the four fingers. Very often this evil can be avoided when playing in positions, by executing the four-finger skip instead of the three-finger, so that instead of using fingers 1, 2, 1, we employ fingers 1, 2, 3, 1. This movement may be used to equal advantage both in going upward or in gliding downward. (See Ex.)

Als Autorität fur die letzten Bemerkungen fuhre ich de beruhmten Virtuosen Charles de Beriot an, welche derselbe auc im zweiten Theile seiner als ausgezeichnet anerkannten grosse Violinschule vertreten hat. Was de Beriot neben seinem Solisten thum auch als Lehrer bedeutete, bezeugen mehrere aus seiner Schul hervorgegangene beruhmte Meister wie Vieuxtemps, Prum Leonard.—Auch L. Spohr vertritt diese Ansicht, indem er in sein grossen Violinschule bezuglich des Abreichens der Tone mit dem und 4, Finger bei Gelegenheit seiner Es-dur Studie in der III. Lag sagt: "Soll der abgerichte Ton mit dem nachstliegenden in eine Strich zusammen gezogen werden, so darf er nur *einen halben To* entfernt liegen, weil bei dem ganzen Ton durch das Zuruckzieh der Finger *ein unangenehmes Heulen* gehort wurde."

Spohr hat aber sowohl bei Bezeichnung seiner Schulstudien auch anderer Violin-Compositionen sehr oft unerwogen gelassen, das dieses so auffallend horbare Gleiten der Finger beim *gebundene* Spiel, wenn *langsamere* Tone aufeinander folgen, stets *beim Lage verkehr* bemerkbar ist, sobald dieser auf dem ganzen Ton ausgefuh wird, und zwar nicht nur beim *Abwartsziehen*, sondern auch bei *Aufwartsgleiten jedes* der vier Finger. Man vermeidet dieses Ueb sehr oft dadurch, dass man beim Lagenspiel statt des Terzensprung den *Quartensprung* eintreten lasst, also statt 1. 2. 1. Finger, wah 1. 2. 3. 1. Finger. Es gilt dieser Wind sowohl fur das Heraufgehe als auch fur das Heruntergleiten. Z. B.

Remark. The advantages shown in the above changes of position are not intended for solo (resp.) quartet-playing. Orchestra players should be firmly impressed with the fact that their special practice also requires a well-studied finger-position, especially in delicate passages. I have attended orchestra rehearsals, at which the absolute necessity of such a condition was most forcibly exemplified. One of our best directors, Anton Rubinstein, in rehearsing one of his own compositions, caused a piano passage to be repeated several times, because some of the players executed a change of position in diverse ways. In consequence of this inequality, certain passages that required peculiar fingering to be played with proper effect, were not clear, but had a blurred effect until the concertmaster prescribed a uniform mode of fingering for all. It is also an erroneous idea that a well-studied fingering in orchestra playing is not absolutely necessary, so long as the performer executes everything and brings it out clearly. Every orchestra player should realize that what may perhaps seem to him to be an unimportant matter, changing position, he must not only be in strict accordance with the others as regards pure intonation, exact rhythm, correct accentuation of the measure, the single notes, the shading of forte and piano, as well as the correct division of the bowstroke, but *also in the fingering*, that he should exactly *accord with the others*. It is therefore the duty of the leading violinist to see that the proper marks are made in all the different parts. Practise has proven that the above fingering, which will prove of the greatest utility in every form of scale practice by changes of position, is repeatedly true in many orchestra passages. Every violinist has been made familiar in his school studies with the four-finger skip, in his practice of the broken triads through two and three octaves. For further development in the direction of scale practice, with which every violinist should preface his daily studies, the Violin Methods of Beriot and Alard are the ones by which the student can most quickly and surely acquire (in single and double-stops) a knowledge of the fingerboard.

As regards the study of the Kreutzer 'Etudes, I would remark that it is *not so much the amount of practise* as it is *how*—or, in other words, the *way and manner* in which it is conducted. One might play etudes from eight to ten hours daily and still not *practise* nor *study* them. The great secret of all quick playing, all rapid execution which the beginner tries to acquire by hurriedly playing through the etudes, can only be successfully accomplished in just the opposite manner; by slow careful practise. I recommend, for instance, to successfully accomplish such a vital and indispensable result that

Anm. Die hier angeführten Vortheile für den Lagenverkehr gelten aber nicht nur für das Solo-resp. Quartettspiel. Auch die Orchesterpraxis verlangt an delicaten Orchesterstellen einen gut überlegten Fingersatz. Habe ich doch einer Orchesterprobe beigewohnt, in welcher einer unserer begabtesten Dirigenten, Anton Rubinstein, bei Einstudirung eines seiner Werke eine Pianostelle des Streichquartetts mehrmals wiederholen liess, weil von einzelnen der Geiger die Fingersätze mit verschiedenem Lagenverkehr ausgeführt worden, und durch diese Uneinigkeit die Stelle nicht durchsichtig wurde, sondern von verwischter Wirkung blieb, bis vom Concertmeister ein allgemein zu merkender Fingersatz vorgeschrieben wurde. Er ist also die Ansicht, dass ein gut durchdachter Fingersatz beim Orchesterspiel nicht gerade Bedingung wäre, wenn er nur Alles träfe und rein herausbrächte, keine richtige. Jeder an einer Stimme fungirende Orchestergeiger muss nicht nur bezüglich der reinen Intonation, der genauen Rhythmik, der Betonung der Tactglieder und der einzelnen Noten, der Nuancen von Forte und Piano, sowie in genauer Eintheilung und Anordnung der Bogenstriche, sondern *auch im Fingersatze genau mit den Andern übereinstimmen.* Es gehört daher mit zu den Functionen des Vorgeigers, für Eintragung bereiter Bezeichnungen in sämmtliche Stimmen zu sorgen. Auch hierbei hat *die Praxis* gelehrt, dass der eben besprochene Fingersatz bezüglich des Lagenverkehrs in vielen Fällen auch für Orchesterpassagen gilt.—Der Quartensprung an und für sich ist jedem Geiger schon durch das Schulstudium bei Gelegenheit des Uebens des gebrochenen Dreiklangs durch zwei und drei Octaven genügend geläufig. Es handelt sich demnach nur um seine weitere Verwerthung. Für das Scalenstudium, das jeder Geiger täglich vor dem Etüden-Studium vor nehmen sollte, sind die Scalen Bezeichnungen in den Violin-Methoden von de Beriot und Alard (beide ersch, bei Schott's Söhne) diejenigen, auf welchen der Studirende am schnellsten und sichersten zu einer reinen und correcten Intonation der Scala (sowohl in einfachen als in Doppelgriffen) und zur Kenntniss des Griffbretts gelangt.

Ueber das Einüben der Kreutzer'schen Etüden selbst bemerke ich für die Interessenten, dass es *nicht so sehr auf das viele Ueben* als auf das "*Wie*," die *Art und Weise des Uebens* ankommt. Man kann acht bis zehn Stunden des Tages Etüden *spielen* und dieselben doch *nicht üben, nicht studiren.* Das grosse Geheimniss alles *schnellen* Spiels, aller rapiden Fertigkeit, welcher der Uneingeweihte durch *schnelles* Einspielen der Etüden mit Erfolg nachzu jagen glaubt, findet seine Lösung gerade im Gegentheil durch *langsames sorgfältiges*

Etude 1 be practised in both the up and the down stroke, with the entire length of the bow. First in slow half-notes. If full, perfect intonation be secured, then in slow quarter-notes, then in slow eighth-notes, and finally in sixteenth-notes, until the Etude can be played in Allegro-tempo, with perfect intonation and with all the notes brought out as clear as a bell.

Ueben. Ich empfehle z. B. bei Etude 1 dieselbe im Herunter— und Heraufstrich mit ganzer Bogenlange folgendermassen zu uben. Zuerst jeden Ton in langsamen halben Noten. Ist in dieser Weise die Intonation vollstandig gesichert, in langsamen Vierteln, dann in langsamen Achteln, schliesslich in Sechzehntheilen, bis die Etude glockenrein im Allegro-Tempo herausgebracht werden kann.

Then follows the study of the different bowings. Through this slow practise one learns to judge of the purity of every tone. It is scarcely necessary to state, perhaps, that these same principles, which have been so thoroughly exemplified, it is hoped, when they are applied to the study of other Etudes, will produce like results. Legato studies in which eight or more sixteenth-notes are grouped under one slur, should be played first detached; also in detached half, quarter, eighth, and finally in sixteenth notes. When one has acquired a full, perfect intonation in this manner, groups of four, eight and even more sixteenth-notes, slurred, may be taken together in one stroke of the bow. (See Ex.)

Darauf erst folge das Studium der verschiedenen Stricharten. Durch dieses langsame Ueben lernt der Betreffende jeden Ton bezuglich seiner Reinheit genau prufen. Es ist wohl kaum zu erwahnen nothig, dass man dieses Verfahren beim Studium der andern Etuden *ebenfalls* mit den hervorgehobenen Vortheilen anwenden kann.—Legato-Etuden, in welchen acht und mehr Sechzehntheile gebunden sind ube man zuerst ohne jede Bindung, also gestossen in halben, Viertel,—Achtel, schliesslich in Sechzehntel-Noten. Wenn man die Intonation in dieser Weise vollstandig beherrscht, binde man Gruppen von vier, acht und mehr Sechzehntel-Noten in einen Strich zusammen. z. B.

Respecting the different Trill-Etudes, I would remark that in order to secure complete purity of tone, it would be well to practise the same without observing any of the trill-marks until the fingers execute the notation, according to the prescribed application, (in Etude 15, 16, 17, 20 and 23 there are two different applications indicated) clear and sure; they may then be studied with the trill.—As it is probable that many students may play the Kreutzer Etudes without the supervision of a teacher, the following hints if carefully observed, will prove very useful to them. The habit of *regular, daily* study is of supreme importance; for instance, do not practise too much one day and very little, or not at all another. Also is it advantageous to practise the same hours each day as it insures *freshness* and energy in the work; but do not, in consequence of long hours of forced study become wearied out. Explanatory remarks concerning bowing, springing-bow, tremolo, trill, fingering and finger-gymnastics, will be found in an appendix later on. When the student has been through this volume to the last Etude; and then through them again until it is possible, perhaps, for him to play them without the notes, he would do well to attempt the transposition of some of the Etudes, a half, or a whole tone, a major or a minor third; also to transpose some of them even an octave higher. The advantages to be derived from the ability to transpose readily at sight, which can be acquired by practice, are very great and cannot be overestimated. This will become more apparent to the young student as he advances with his study, and especially when, later on, the necessity for it arises professionally, as is very often the case.

Bezuglich der verschiedenen Triller-Etuden bemerke ich, dass man, um sich einer vollstandigen Reinheit zu vergewissern, wohl daran thut, jede derselben zuerst ohne die verzeichneten Triller zu uben, und erst, wenn man sie in den vorgeschriebenen Applicaturen (bei Etude 15, 16, 17, 20 u. 23 sind in dieser Ausgabe zwei verschiedene Applicaturen vermerkt) rein und sicher ausfuhren kann und sie in den Fingern hat, studire man dieselben mit den Trillern. —Da manche Interessenten die Kreutzer'schen Etuden, wie erwahnt, vielleicht ohne Lehrer studiren, wird ihnen die genaue Befolgung dieser Winke gewiss von Nutzen sein. Es moge noch hinzugefugt werden, dass *tagliches regelmassiges* Ueben von Wichtigkeit ist, dass nicht z. B. den einen Tag sehr viel, den andern wieder sehr wenig oder gar nicht geubt werde. Auch ist es vortheilhaft, in seiner Tages-ordnung bestimmte Stunden fur das Ueben festzusetzen, damit man stets mit der nothigen *Frische* und *Energie* an's Werk gehe und sich auch nicht durch zu forcirtes langstundiges Ueben ubermude. Ueber Stricharten, Springbogen, Tremolo, Triller, Fingersatze, Fingergymnastik finden sich in den am Schlusse befindlichen Anmerkungen Erlauterungen.—Hat der Studirende diese Ausgabe bis zu den letzten dieser Etuden mehrere Male durchgemacht, so dass er selbige moglichst *auswendig* spielen kann, so wird er wohl daran thun, Transpositions-Versuche derselben zu unternehmen, indem er einzelne der Etuden einen halben, einen ganzen Ton, eine kleine oder grosse Terz, einige auch eine Octave hoher transponirt.—It redactioneller Beziehung noch die Bemerkungen, dass diese Ausgaben 42 Etuden bringt, welche sammtlich von Rudolph Kreutzer

n editing these new markings I desire to observe that the Etudes in ^ sind. Mir lag kein Grund vor, Etude 14 (dreistimmige Arpeggien) is edition are all by Rudolph Kreutzer. I know of no reason why und Etude 21 (getrennte Octaven behandelnd) fortzulassen, wie dieude 14 (3 part arpeggios) and Etude 21 (treating separate octaves) ses in andern Ausgaben stattgefunden hat. Auch findet man hould be left out as has been done in some other editions. One Ausgaben, in welchen Etude 25, das Adagio sostenuto (für langathso finds editions in which Etude 25, the Adagio sostenuto (for mige Bogenfuhrung und das Studium des langen Trillers berechnet), ng bowings and the study of the long trills), and further, also, und ferner auch Etude 26 (ein Adagio, welches ein Beispiel von der ude 26 (an Adagio which presents an example of superior skill bedeutenden Gewandheit bietet, welche die alten Meister im Einso, in which the old master interwove ornamental runs with the flechten von Laufern beim Adagio-Vortrag besassen,) fehlen. Vieldagio-portion) are missing. Moreover I have added to Etude 14 mehr habe ich zu Etude 14 und Etude 21 noch ein Verzeichniss von nd Etude 21 a list of bowings and variations the practical utility of Stricharten und Varianten gefugt, welche sich in der Praxis bewahrt hich has been abundantly proven. haben.

Frankfort on the Main, November, 1884.

EMIL KROSS.

Frankfurt a M im November 1884.

EMIL KROSS.

RUDOLPH KREUTZER.

Among the names that are famous in violin-history, none are more familar to ambitious students of that instrument than that of the celebrated artist, virtuoso and composer, Rudolph Kreutzer. Born at Versailles, Nov. 16, 1766, and endowed with great natural talent, he began the study of the violin at a very early age under the tuition of his father who was a practical musician of ability, supplemented y instruction from Stamitz a noted violinist of that time. Besides practising the violin, young Kreutzer, following the promptings of his musical tendencies, had composed many pieces even before he had acquired a theoretical knowledge of the rules of harmony. At the age of 16 his violin playing was so remarkable that it had engaged the attention of Marie Antoinette, and this secured for him the position of first violin in the Chapelle du Roi. The many opportunities which he then enjoyed of hearing the two great violinists Mestrino and Viotti, ad such a stimulating effect upon his talent that he rapidly improved in his own execution and style of playing. He next received the appointment of solo-violinist at the Theatre Italien where he subsequently produced several operas of his own composition.

In 1797 he made a professional tour through Germany, Italy and the Netherlands, the brilliancy and individuality of his playing everywhere creating the greatest enthusiasm and admiration. In 1798 Kreutzer resided in Vienna where he was appointed "First Violin of the Academy of Arts and of the Imperial Chamber Music." Upon his return to Paris and to the Conservatory where he had been professor of the violin from the foundation of that institution, he and the celebrated violinist Rode collaborated the famous "Method de Violin" for the use of the students. Kreutzer frequently appeared at concerts as a soloist, and the performance of his "Duos Concertantes" with Rode were always considered a brilliant attraction. In 1801, when Rode went to Russia, Kreutzer became first solo-violin at the Grand Opera, which again gave him the opportunity to produce successively several new operas and ballets. In 1802, Napoleon as First Consul appointed him first-violin of the Chapelle, and in 1806 his title became "Solo-Violin to the Emperor." When Louis XVIII. regained the throne of France in 1815 he made him Maitre de la Capelle. Kreutzer became Vice-conductor of the Academy in 1816, and the following year, Conductor-in-chief, which position be retained until 1824, in which year he was made a Chevalier of the Legion of Honor. A serious and permanent injury to one of his arms now obliged him to relinquish violin-playing, and in 1825 he retired from the Conservatory. An apoplectic attack which subsequently rendered him a confirmed invalid and greatly impaired his mind, resulted in a gradual decline that terminated his life at the age of 65, on the 6th of June, 1831, at Geneva.

Of the four great representative masters of the classical Violin-School of Paris, VIOTTI, RODE, KREUTZER and BALLIOT, the third place in the order of development is accorded by competent authority to Kreutzer, whose style, judged on the basis of his violin-concertos, while it appears on the whole more brilliant than Rode's, is considered less modern than that of Balliot. Although Kreutzer composed 39 operas and ballets, all of which were produced in Paris; and published no less than 19 Violin-Concertos; also duos, and 2 symphonies concertantes for 2 violins; numerous etudes and caprices for violin solo; sonatas for violin and cello; 15 trios and a symphonie concertante for 2 violins and cello; 15 string quartets; and several airs with variations, his fame, as time has proved, must ever rest on his unsurpassed work the "42 Etudes for the Violin," which, it has well been said, "occupies a unique position in the literature of violin studies." The fact that it has been recognized and adopted by the best masters of all schools, irrespective of nationality, as the basis of a solid execution on the violin, furnishes incontrovertable proof of its unequalled superiority. As such it will long remain, a guide to students everywhere and an imperishable monument to the genius of its author.—EDITOR.

EXPLANATION OF THE SIGNS:

⊓ = Down-Stroke.
V = Up Stroke.
w. B. = Whole Bow.
h. B. u. = Upper half of the Bow.
h. B. l. = Lower half of the Bow.
Pt. = At the Point of the Bow.
M. = In the Middle.
Fr. = At the Frog.
Th. = A Third part of the Bow.
u. Th. = Upper Third of the Bow.
l. Th. = Lower Third of the Bow.
I. = E - String.
II. = A - String.
III. = D - String.
IV. = G - String.

1.
2.
3.
4. } 1st. 2d. 3d. or 4th. Finger remaining upon *one* string during the time value of the note.

1.
1.
2.
2.
3.
3. } 1st. 2d. 3d. Finger remaining upon *two* strings during the time value of the notes.

♩ etc. In stopped Fifths, one note silent.

⁓ = Tremolo of the Fingers.

ERKLÄRUNG DER ZEICHEN:

⊓ = *Herunterstrich.*
V = *Aufstrich.*
g. B. = *ganzer Bogen.*
h. B. o. = *halber Bogen oben.*
h. B. u. = *halber Bogen unten.*
Sp. = *an der Spitze.*
M. = *in der Mitte.*
Fr. = *am Frosch.*
Dr. = *Drittheil des Bogens.*
ob. Dr. = *oberes Drittheil des Bogens.*
un. Dr. = *unteres Drittheil des Bogens.*
I. = *E - Saite.*
II. = *A - Saite.*
III. = *D - Saite.*
IV. = *G - Saite.*

1.
2.
3.
4. } *1. 2. 3. oder 4. Finger während der Dauer der Punkte auf einer Saite liegen lassen*

1.
1.
2.
2.
3.
3. } *1. 2. 3. Finger während der Dauer der Punkte auf zwei Saiten liegen lassen.*

♩ etc. *im Quintgriff stumm zu greifende Noten.*

⁓ = *Bebung des Fingers.*

42 ETÜDEN von RUDOLPH KREUTZER.

Etude 1. The first 36 Bowings will familiarize one with both the Down- and Up-strokes of the bow.
Die ersten 36 Stricharten fange man sowohl mit dem Herunter- als auch mit dem Aufstrich an.

In 31) start at the Frog and for every group of quarter notes employ one eighth of the bow-length till the Point is reached; with the same stroke and in the same way proceed backwards from the Point to the Frog.
Bei 31) setzt man am Frosch an und verbraucht zu jeder Quartole ein Achtel der Bogenlänge, bis man zur Spitze gelangt ist, darauf streiche man in derselben Weise von der Spitze zum Frosch zurück.

Etüde 2.

This bowing is to be thoroughly studied, as a great mastery of the bow will thereby be obtained
Diese Strichart ist viel zu studiren, da sie eine grosse Herrschaft über den Bogen verschafft.

martelé

The Staccato must first be very thoroughly studied, all the notes being evenly executed with a swinging hand, so that the bow does not leave the string. The first and last notes should be given an energetic accent, while the others should be heard struck out in even pushes of the bow. A study in this manner is the surest means of acquiring dexterity in these strokes of the bow.

Das Staccato muss man erst sehr langsam studren, mit ungezwungener Hand alle Noten gleichmäsig abstossen, so dass der Bogen sich nie von der Sa entferne, auf die erste und letzte Note einen Nac druck legen, während die andern in gleichmässig martellirenden Stössen zu Gehör gebracht werden Diese Manier zu studiren, ist das sicherste, Mitt die Geschicklichkeit dieses Bogenstriches zu erlang

Etüde 3.

Etüde 4 is to be studied Allegro moderato, at first, afterwards Allegro, and finally in Presto tempo. a) each measure with one bow-stroke, b) two measures with one bow-stroke. This Etude is for daily practice to impart strength and evenness of action to the fingers; it is also equally useful as a preparation to the exercises for the study of the trill which follow later.

Etüde 4 ist zuerst Allegro moderato, später im Allegro, schliesslich im Presto-Tempo zu studiren. a) jeden Tact auf einen Bogenstrich, b) zwei Tacte auf einen Bogenstrich. Diese Etüde ist täglich zu üben, weil selbige sehr zur Kräftigung und Unabhängigkeit der Finger beiträgt und zugleich als gute Vorstudie zu den später folgenden Trillerübungen zu benutzen ist.

Etüde 4.
Allegro moderato.

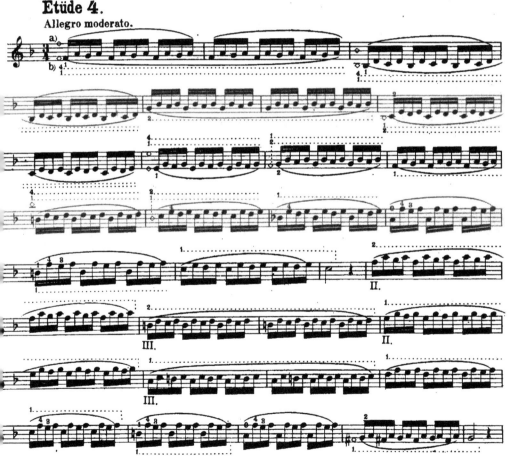

xercise can be played with the same bowing usly given in Etude 1. At * *do not leave the 1st.* *on the string* at each upward movement of the ger, but move it backward after the higher po- is attained. Two other very important finger- f this Etude will be found in the remarks at d. (Page 91.

*Diese Uebung kan mit denselben Stricharten wie Etüde 1 vorgetragen werden. Von * ab verlässt der erste Fin- ger die Saite nicht und rückt bei jedem Höherschreit- en des vierten Finger um eine Lage höher. Zwei noch sehr wichtige Fingersätze zu dieser Etüde in den An- merkungen am Schlusse. (Saite 91.*

Etüde 5.
Allegro moderato.

(Etude 6 is also to be practised at the Frog; further, with the entire bow-length passed quickly over the string.) In Etude 6 and 7 the peculiar bowing is the socalled Martelé, (hammered) and consists in energetic strokes at the Point of the bow. All the notes must be strongly and clearly produced, and be of equal duration. Yet the tones must be well separated one from the other, a little pause occuring after each note; accordingly *Etude 6* should sound like the following:

(*Etüde 6 auch am Frosch zu üben; ferner mit ganzer genlänge die Saite schnell durchziehen.*) Der bei Etü und 7 anzuwendende Strich ist das sogenannte Mart (*gehämmert*). Er besteht in energischen Stössen an der tze des Bogens. Alle Noten müssen kräftig, doch sauber gestrichen werden und von gleicher Dauer sein. Doch m man, um die Töne recht von einander abzusondern, eine ne Pause hinter jeder Note eintreten lassen, demnach wi die Klangwirkung von Etude 6 *diese sein*:

and in Etude 7:
and bei

In the pause between the notes, the bow, therefore, must remain still an instant without pressure. Then, as it naturally requires more effort to produce the notes in the Up bow-stroke than those in the Down-stroke, a stronger pressure must consequently be imparted to them. It is also recommended to study this Etude quite slowly at first. (see Preface.)

In the higher tones on the E string the Martelé-stroke must be lengthened somewhat, so that the inequalities which exist between the tones may be rendered imperceptible; yet the general character of this bowing must not be changed, and the little pause between the notes must always be noticeable.

Bei der Pause zwischen den Noten muss daher der Bo ohne Druck bleiben und einen Moment still stehen. Da Noten im Heraufstrich natürlich schwerer zu marki sind als diejenigen im Herunterstrich, so muss man demselben einen kräftigern Druck ausüben. Auch bei ser Etude ist natürlich zuerst ein ganz langsames E studiren zu empfehlen. (s. Vorwort.)

Bei den hohen Tönen auf der E-Saite verlängert m den Martelé-Strich etwas, um die Dünnheit derselben den andern Tönen auszugleichen; jedoch darf das Char teristische dieses Striches hierdurch nicht abgeschwä werden und muss die kleine Pause zwischen den No immer merkbar sein.

Etüde 6.

e springing over the strings must be effected with eat dexterity of the wrist, without direct co-operation of the elbow and upper part of the arm.

Das Uebersrpingen der saiten ist mit der grössten Geschmeidigkeit des Handgelenks auszuführen; directe Mitwirkung des Ellbogens und Oberarms zu vermeiden.

Etüde 7.

Allegro assai. Same stroke as in foregoing example.
(Strich wie im vorigen Beispiel.)

This Etude is also to be studied with Spiccato-stroke jumping in even 16th. notes and decidedly piano. Thereby every note of this arpeggio Etude is to be played clear and round; between each note a little pause should be heard.*) In bowing 24, the second 32d. note is to be played with a longer up-stroke; for by this means the division of the bow for sustaining the long notes is to be regulated. Be careful that the Rhythm is not disturbed.

Diese Etüde ist auch mit Spiccato-Strich hüpfend in gleichmässigen 16 teln und zwar im piano zu studiren. Dabei ist jede Note dieser arpeggioartigen Etüde sauber und rund anzustreichen, indem zwischen jeder Note eine ganz kleine Pause hörbar wird.*) Bei Strichart 2 ist für das zweite 32tel ein längerer Aufstrich anzuwenden, wodurch die Bogeneintheilung für das Aushalten der langen Note regulirt wird; jedoch darf hierdurch der Rhythmus nicht gestört werden.

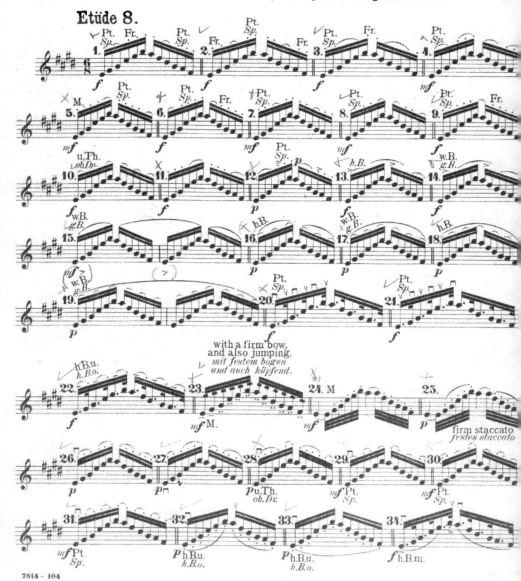

In Bowing I) attack the string with a sudden, forte-stroke, employing the whole bow-length, then executing 6 notes broadly, in thrusts, at the point of the bow, and then, again, following the forte-stroke with 6 broad strokes at the Frog. In Bowing II) use for the forte-stroke only one half of the bow, and taking the 6 thrust notes the first time at the Point, and the next time in the same way in the middle of the bow. In Bowing III) double the quickness of the notes in the *two* $\frac{2}{4}$ measures by giving each note, excepting the first and eighth, *two* strokes. In Bowing IV) give *three* strokes to each note, excepting the first and the eighth note.

Bei Strichart I) durchschneide man die Saite mit einem schnellen Fortestrich, indem man die ganze Bogenlänge gebraucht, stösst 6 Noten breit a.d.Sp. dann folgt wieder der Fortestrich worauf man 6 breite Striche am Frosche executirt. Bei Strichart II) verbrauche man zum Fortestrich nur den halben Bogen und führe die 6 gestossenen Noten einmal an d.Spitze, das andere Mal in der Mitte aus. Bei Strichart III) verdoppele man die Geschwindigkeit und führe auf $\frac{2}{4}$ zwei Tacte aus, indem man jede Note mit Ausnahme der ersten und achten zwei Mal anstreicht. Bei IV) streicht man jede Note mit Ausnahme der ersten und achten Note drei Mal an.

18. By this Legato-Etude great care must be taken to acquire perfect evenness of the 16th notes and also ease and elegance in the motions of the right wrist.

Bei dieser Legato-Etüde achte man genau auf grösste Gleichmässigkeit der Sechzehntheile, und auf leichte, elegante Biegungen des rechten Handgelenke.

Etüde 10.

Etude 11 as a preparatory study for a fine execution of the Cantilena is of particular importance and is to be studied with the fingering indicated both above and below. It is, however, the lower fingering that is preferable, since in the movement of the hand which usually reaches the *next following* position by a downward glide, the little jumps, as in the upper fingering, also, are consequently less audible. (See Preface on this) The changes of position should be easily and quickly made.

Etüde 11 ist als *Vorstudium* für eine schöne Ausführung der Cantilenen von besonderer Wichtigkeit und sowohl mit dem obern als mit dem untern Fingersatze zu studiren. ist jedoch der untere vorzuziehen, weil bei demselben die Hand gewöhnlich mer in die nächst folgende *Lage* bei Hinunter-Gleiten geht, mithin die Sprünge kleiner als bei obern Fingersatze sind und demnach auch weniger hörb (S. hierüber Vorwort.) Der Lagenwechsel gehe leicht und schnell von Statten.

Etüde 11.

Etüde 12.

In this Legato-Etude control with great precision the right wrist in order to obtain excellent results relative to the Legato.

Bei dieser Legato-Etüde controlire man mit der grössten Genauigkeit das rechte Handgelenk, um ein schönes Resultat bezüglich des Legato zu erzielen.

Etude 18 is to be studied forte and with boldness in all the passages, so that the same strength of tone will be evenly maintained throughout the three octaves, and not be perceptibly weakened (in the 3d octave) at the bridge.

Etüde 13 ist im Forte zu studiren und müssen die Passagen mit Kühnheit herauskommen, sowie die Tonstärke durch alle drei Octaven eine gleichmässige sein muss und nicht nach dem Stege zu (in der dritten Octave) abnehmen darf.

BOWINGS AND VARIATIONS TO ETUDE 14.
STRICHARTEN UND VARIANTEN ZU ETÜDE 14.

3. Of the 50 Arpeggio-Bowings the first 19 may also be practised beginning with the up bow.
Von den 50 Arpeggio-Stricharten kann man die ersten 19 auch mit den Heraufstrich beginnend üben.

Here the student through the practise of the various Arpeggio-figures will probably find the *best* means to render the wrist free, flexible and steady; following these are other Arpeggio-figures which by beginning with the Down-stroke as well as with the Up-stroke (at the Point, in the Middle and at the Frog) will ensure expertness. It is also advantageous, with conscientious bowing, to review the *Spiccato-stroke* of the previous page, and even to transpose the Etude-figures. The student will also find a great deal therein that is pleasing and useful by inventing *new* forms at each review, and by transposing the figures, and in reproducing them in quartolet as well as in triplet groups.

Da der Studirende durch das Ueben der verschiedenten Arpeggio-Figuren wohl die beste Gelegenheit fin sein Handgelenk locker, geschmeidig und ausdauernd z machen, folgen hier noch einige Arpeggio-Figuren, welc sowohl mit Herunter-als mit Heraufstrich beginnend (an Spitze, in der Mitte und am-Frosch) geübt werden könn Auch ist es vortheilhaft, im Spiccatostrich und mit gewi Stricharten der vorigen Seite die Umkehrungen und V setzungen der Etüdenfiguren zu üben. Auch wird der St dirende darin Vergnügen und Nutzen finden, in angege ener Weise neue Umkehrungen und Verzetzungen der F uren und zwar sowohl in Quartolen-als in Triolen-Gr pen zu erfinden.

Etüde 14. (All 3 strings are to be stopped simultaneously, fully and firmly.)
(Alle 3 saitigen Griffe sind sofort vollständig zu bringen und festzuhalten.)
This Etude presents the same principles that were recommended in Etude 10.
Bei dieser Etüde gilt ebenfalls, was bereits bei Etüde 10 empfohlen wurde.

ginnig with the *under* tone one trill movement.   With two trill-strokes.
untern *Ton anfangend mit einem Trillerschlag.*   *Mit zwei Trillerschlägen.*

ginnig with the *upper* tone one trill movement.   With two trill-strokes.
obern *Ton anfangend mit einem Trillerschlag.*   *Mit zwei Trillerschlägen.*

this and in the following trill-studies it is   *In dieser und den folgenden Triller- Etüden ist so-*
to practise the fingering indicated both a-   *wohl der obere als auch der untere Fingersatz zu*
and below.   *üben.*

Etüde 16.
Moderato.

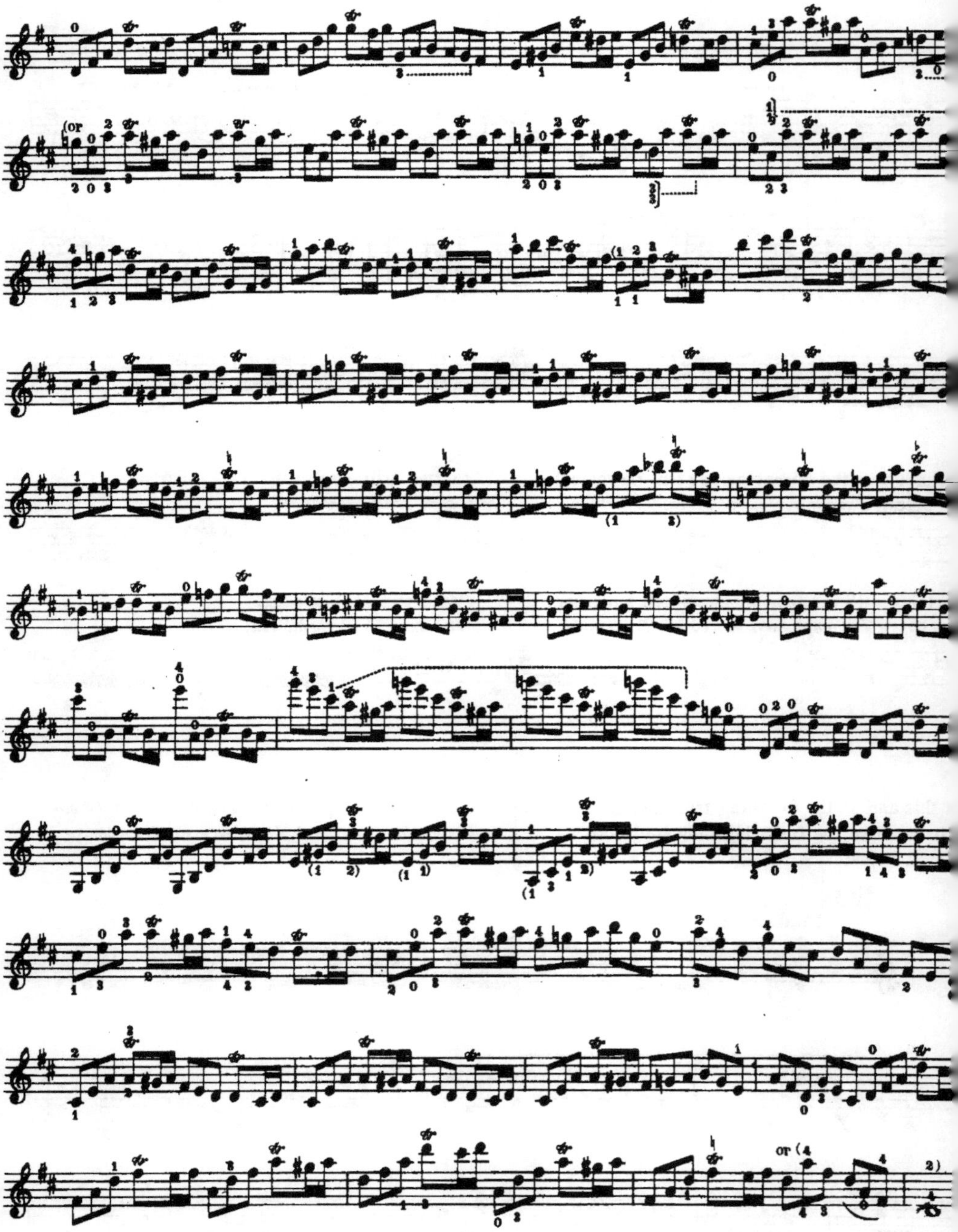
(or
or

That the player may not be wearied by too many successive trill-studies, the 8 by Kreutzer which treat this subject have been interrupted by 2 Etudes presenting other technicalities.

Um den Spieler nicht durch zu viele auf einander f gende Trillerstudien zu ermüden, sind 8 Kreutzer'sc diesen Gegenstand behandelnden Nummern durch 2 E den über andere technische Manieren unterbrochen wor

Etüde 18.
Before studying Number 18, review Bowing 18 of Etude 1.
Vor dem Studium von Nummer 18 übe man Strichart 18 aus Etude 1.

33

38

As various bowings and variations thereof may be adapted to this Etude with excellent results, several have been added in this edition. Still before proceeding one must attain accuracy in octave intonation as the least deviation in unisons from pure intonation is very disagreeable to the musical ear when octaves are played. Then proceed with certainty in a series of octaves by not raising the 2d. & 3d. fingers, as they furnish support to the 1st. & 4th. fingers by means of their contact. Study Etude, 1) martelé beginning with the Down as well as the Up-stroke. a) at the Point b) at the Frog c) hopping-stroke in the middle of the bow. 2) Legato 1 & 2, 3 & 4, slurred 16th. notes, taking care that the first of the two slurred notes is not played too short. A close observation of the right wrist is necessary. 3) Legato in the 2d. & 3d, 4th. & 1st. slurred 16th. notes, which must be played piano as the shifting of the hand will then be less audible (in the Bowing are the necessary indications) 4) with the Viotti Bowing (also indications) 5) fouetté (whipped) beginning with the Up-stroke.

Da diese Etüde sich zu verschiedenen Stricharten u. auch zu Varianten ganz vortrefflich eignet, ist diesel auch, mit diesen versehen, anbei gedruckt worden. Jedo gehe man an diese dann, renn man in der Octaven-Intona tion vollständig sicher ist, da ausser bei Unisono-Griff bei keinem Intervall auch die geringste Abweichung von reinen Intonation dem Ohre so weh thut, als beim Octavens Daher hebe man zur Sicherheit bei fortschreitenden Octa den 2. u. 3. Finger nicht auf, damit diese Finger dem 1. u. 4. Fi eine Stütze in der Berührung mit ihnen bieten. Man stud diese Etüde 1) martelé sowohl mit dem Ab-als mit dem A strich beginnend. a) an der Spitze b) am Frosch c) hüpfen Strich in der Mitte des Bogens. 2) Legato 1. u. 2, 3. u. 4. Sec zehntheil bindend, und gebe man genau Achtung dass das te der beiden gebundenen Sechzehntheile nicht zu kurz spielt werde. Eine sorgfältige Beobachtung des rechten Ha gelenks ist nothwendig. 3) Legato, indem man 2. u. 3tes. 4. 1stes Sechzehntheil bindet, und zwar piano, weil dabei d Fortrücken der Hand weniger hörbar ist, (diese Strichart anbei ausgeschrieben) 4) mit der Viotti'schen Strichart (eb falls ausgeschrieben) 5) fouetté (gepeitscht) mit dem Aufstr beginnend.

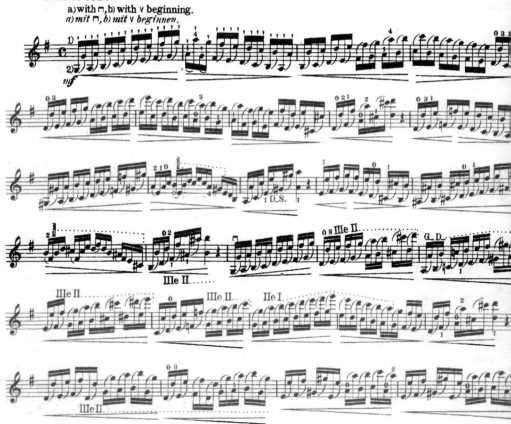

VARIATIONS to ETUDE 21.
VARIANTEN zu ETUDE 21.

Etüde 22.

43

Etüde 23.

45

46

Etüde 24.

In executing the Trill in exact rhythmical division, and in the production of the Trill-stroke first in 32d. notes and to attain skill and surety in 64th. notes.—Practise the Scale-figures of this Etude, after they have been rendered perfectly clear and even in 16th. notes, also in 32d. notes. Then at the F in measure 71, count 5 eighth notes and play the descending scale in regular, even 32d. notes. In a similar way the student should also divide the measures 75, 79, 99, 100 and 107 in this Etude.

Bei Ausführung der Triller achte man auf genaue rhythmische Eintheilung und führe die Trillerschläge zuerst in Zweiunddreissigtheilen und nach erlangter Fertigkeit u. Sicherheit in Vierundsechzigtheilen aus.—Die Scalen-Figuren der Etüde. übe man, wenn dieselben in Sechzehntheilen vollständig rein und gleichmässig gelingen, auch in Zweiunddreissigtheilen. Demnach wären auf das f. im 71 Tact 5 Achtel zu zählen und die herablaufende Scala in regelmässigen Zweiunddreissigtheilen zu spielen. In ähnlicher Weise rechne der Studirende sich die Eintheilung der Tacte 75, 79, 99, 100 und 107 dieser Etüde aus.

Etüde 25. (See note P. 82.)
(siehe Anmerkung S. 82.)

50

he student will do well, after he has studied the preling Adagio, to go on to the following mode: First card the written bowings and nuances; in each separate measure take two or more bow-strokes and play passages with equal strength of tone; give the ups of notes exactly the same rhythmical division do not play ad libitum.— Adjust the rhythmical ision in the following manner: Count Eighths slowly I play first the groups of eight notes (octolets) in n 32d. notes; then the first measure will sound follows:

Der Studirende wird wohl daran thun, wenn er beim Studium des vorstehenden Adagio auf folgende Weise verfährt. Zuerst halte man sich nicht an die vorgeschriebenen Bogenstriche und Nüancen, sondern nehme auf jeden Takt zwei und mehr Bogenstriche und spiele die Passagen in gleichmässiger Tonstärke, indem die Notengruppen rhythmisch genau eintheilt und nicht ad libitum spielt.— Die rhythmische Eintheilung geschehe in folgender Weise: Man zähle langsame Achtel und spiele zuerst die Octolengruppen in gleichmässigen Zweiunddreissigtheilen, demnach würde der erste Takt folgendermassen klingen:

y the fifth measure with triplet groups, in even h. notes:

den fünften Takt in Triolengruppen spiele man in gleichmässigen Sechzehntheilen.

ter, at the sustained *b* (Fermata) in the first measure, count *four* Eights, and play the 4 groups of 8 tes as even 64th. notes. At the sustained *d* in measure 5 count *four* Eighths and play the 8 triplet-groups even 32d. notes. In like manner the student should kon each measure of the Adagio. After fully acquiring purity, dexterity and equality in these passages, the same must be played in "pearl" runs. The rality of the runs may also be increased, since at B in e first measure, on *b* six Eighth notes may be counted d then the following run be executed on the last two ghths of the measure; the other measures may also divided in this manner. If one has completely mased the technicalities of this Etude the execution the bowing will be clearly apparent to him. The crescendo and decrescendo signs must be carefully observed and the bow delicately started at the Frog. Be onomical in the use of the bow-length throughout, thereby it will not be too quickly finished.

Später zähle man auf das Fermaten b des ersten Taktes vier Achtel und spiele die vier Octolengruppen in gleichmässigen Vierundsechzigtheilen. Auf das Fermaten d in Takt 5 zähle man vier Achtel und spiele die acht Triolengruppen in gleichmässigen Zweiunddreissigtheilen. In ähnlicher Weise rechne sich der Studirende jeden einzelnen Takt des Adagio aus. Nach erlangter vollkommner Reinheit, Fertigkeit und Gleichmässigkeit in den Passagen müssen dieselben wie Perlen rollen. Man kann alsdann die Geschwindigkeit der Läufer noch steigern, indem man z.B. auf das b im 1ten Takt 6 Achtel zählt und den darauf folgenden Läufer auf die beiden letzten Achtel des Taktes einflechtet und auch in dieser Weise die andern Takte eintheilt. Ist man der Technik in dieser Etüde vollständig sicher, so richte man sein Augenmerk auf die Bogenführung. Man achte genau auf die Crescendo und Decrescendo-Zeichen und sehe sich beim zarten Ansetzen des Bogens am Frosche vor. Man halte mit der Bogenlänge gut Haus, damit man nicht zu früh mit derselben fertig wird.

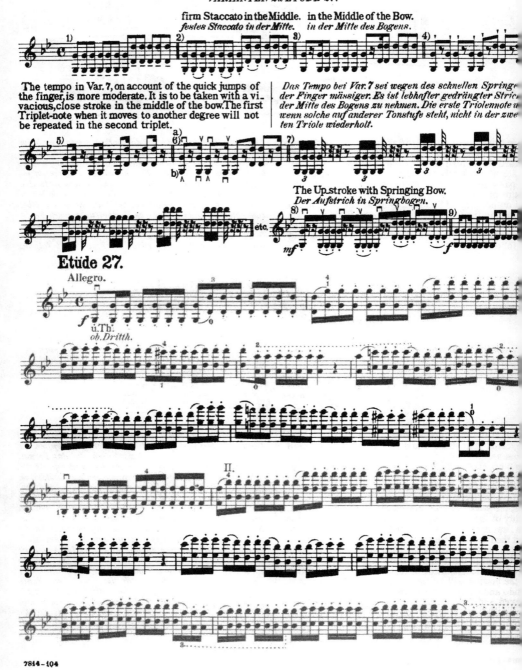

This Etude is to be studied first without the indicated bowing, in simple detached strokes, and afterwards with the written slurring. It will also be useful to transfer and unite with this the registered bowing in Etude I.

Diese Etüde ist zuerst ohne die verzeichneten Strarten im einfachen Detaché-Strich zu studiren, dar mit den vorgeschriebenen Bindungen. Auch ist es von tzen, einige der bei Etüde 1 registrirten Stricharten a dieselbe zu übertragen.

This short Solo-piece may be studied after one has attained the necessary mastery of the bowing therein indicated, also a fine execution with which to enliven it. Count by eighth notes.

Dies kurze Solostück suche man, nachdem man über darin verzeichnete Bogenführung die nöthige Gewandheit erlangt hat, auch durch einen schönen Vortrag zu leben. Man zähle Achtel.

58

In Etude 30 one must be careful that the stretching out of the 3rd. & 4th. fingers is neatly accomplished, while the 1st. finger remains down, the same injunction naturally applies to all other similar pieces in this Etude where the same movement is required. In Paganini's "Art of Playing the Violin" by Guhr, (Schott, Mainz) may be gathered a knowledge of the so-called *"Stechnen"* (sticking) stroke.

Man achte bei Etüde 30 wohl darauf, die Spannung des 3. und 4. Fingers in Takt 40 sehr sauber abzunehmen, während der 1. Finger liegen bleibt; dasselbe gilt natürlich auch von allen übrigen in dieser Etüde vorkommenden Spannungen. Man lese in "Paganini's Kunst, die Violin spielen" von Guhr (Schott, Mainz) über das sogenannte "Stechen" nach.

In this Etude one should be very careful that the first of the two 16th. notes are not played too short, and thereby made to sound somewhat like an appoggiatura. Furthermore, it is advisable every time before the study of this Etude, to practise a chromatic scale in various positions.

Remark: A bowing that frequently occurs in Spohr's Violin compositions, is the one following Etude 31b) (which, however is to be played in moderato tempo.) After every group of the two slurred notes in one stroke, the bow is to be slightly lifted.

Bei dieser Etüde achte man sorgfältig darauf, dass das te der beiden gebundenen Sechzehntheile nicht zu kurz a geführt und demnach etwa wie ein Vorschlag in der Ausf ung klingt. Ferner ist es vortheilhaft, jedes Mal vor dem S dium dieser Etüde zuerst einige chromatische Tonleitern verschiedenen Lagen zu üben.

Anmerkung: Eine Strichart, welcher man sehr häufig i Spohr'schen Violin-Compositionen begegnet, ist nachfolge auf Etüde 31b) übertragen (dieselbe jedoch im Moderato T po zu spielen.) Nach jeder zweiten der auf einen Strich bindenden Noten ist der Bogen etwas zu lüften.

Etüde 31.ª

Etüde 31b.
Allegro moderato.

Etude 32 must be practised daily, as this will impart to the fingers extraordinary vigor and independence. The fingers should be kept down as much as possible, as is shown in the first measure. The first group of quarter notes is taken crescendo; the second decrescendo. Every third and fourth group are to be taken likewise.

Etüde 32 muss täglich geübt werden, da selbige ausserordentlich zur Kräftigung und Unabhängigkeit der Finger beiträgt. Die Finger lasse man so viel als möglich liegen, wie es in den ersten Takten angezeigt ist. Die erste Quartolengruppe nehme man crescendo, die zweite decrescendo; das gleiche findet bei jeder dritten und vierten Quartolengruppe statt.

Etüde 32.
Moderato.

This Etude, in its turn is to be considered a short Solo-piece. It must be rendered throughout in a precise, energetic manner, and with absolute strictness of rhythm. The dotted 8th. notes with the next following 16th. notes are to be executed in the following manner:

Diese Etüde ist wiederum als ein kurzes Solostück zu betrachten. Im Vortrage muss ein sehr bestimmter energischer Charakter und eine strenge Rhythmik durchgeführt werden. Die Ausführung der punctirten Achtel mit nachfolgendem Sechzehntheil ist folgender massen zu executiren:

Therefore after each 8th. note there must occur a sixteenth rest. As more coloring is obtainable in this piece through various bow-strokes, still a second bowing with dotted 8th. notes is presented:

Also hinter jedem Achtel tritt eine Sechzehntheil pause ein. Um dem Stücke durch die Verschiedenheit des Striches mehr Colorit zu geben, ist noch eine zweite Strichart bei den punctirten Achteln angeführt:

This may be changed by employing it with the first alternately.

Dieselbe kann man abwechselnd mit der ersten anwenden.

68

This study should be practised, first, with four notes to one stroke of the bow, in very slow time; stop with the utmost accuracy as regards pure intonation, to obtain which one is advised to be guided often by the open strings. When in this manner the intonation has been rendered pure and full, eight notes may be taken to one bow-stroke in faster time.

Man übe diese Studie zuerst mit je vier Noten auf ein Strich in sehr langsamen Tempo, halte mit der grössten wissenhaftigkeit auf vollkommen reine Intonation, wobei oft die blanken Saiten zu Rathe ziehe. Erst wenn in dieser se die Intonation vollkommen gesichert erscheint, nehme je acht Noten auf einen Strich in bewegterem Tempo.

Etüde 34.

7814-104

One should strictly observe an advantageous position of the hand in order to be able accurately to execute the frequent overreaching of the fourth finger.

Man beobachte stets eine ausgezeichnete Handhaltung, um das öfters eintretende Uebergreifen des vierten Fingers genau ausführen zu können.

Etüde 35.
Andante

70 In practising the so-called Viotti bowing on *double stops*, it is naturally presupposed that one has fully become master of this bowing on *single tones*. This Etude, should first be practised *without* the Viotti bowing in firm Martele-strokes and when the stops are produced clear sure and facile, with the Viotti bowing.

Bei Anwendung der sogenañten Viotti'schen Stric art auf **Doppelgriffe** *ist es natürlich Voraussetzu dass man dieser effectvollen Strichart im einstimm gen Spiele vollständig Herr ist. Man übe diese Etü zuerst* **ohne** *die Viotti'sche Strichart in festen Marte Strichen und dann, wenn man die Griffe ganz rei sicher und geläufig bringt, mit der Viotti'schen Str art.*

Etüde 36.
Allegretto.

71

72. Bring out well the Crescendo at the two slurred notes, and employ the whole length of the bow, so that the two detached sixteenth notes can be taken at the Point and at the Frog alternately.

Man bringe das Crescendo der beiden gebundenen Noten gut heraus und verwende dazu die ganze Bogenlänge, so dass die beiden gestossenen Sechzehntheile einmal an der Spitze und dann am Frosch treten.

Etüde 37.

73

74 Be careful in the changes of position that the Triplets are executed in a correct, round and rolling manner.

Man achte wohl darauf, dass auch in den Applicaturn die *Triolen* recht rund und rollend herauskommen.

Etüde 38.

Etüde 39.

The Fugue Etude 40 can be studied in two different ways: 1) the Eighth notes with the firmly marked martelé-stroke, and the Eighths with concise, detached bowing 2) with the middle of the bow; the Eighths with tossed, marked Spiccato-bowing and the groups of 16th notes with softer Spiccato-bowing.

Die Fuge Etüde 40 kann in zwei verschiedenen Manieren studirt werden: 1) indem man die Achtel mit fest markirten Martelé-Strichen und die Achtel in gedrängten Detaché-Strichen spielt. 2) mit dem mittlern Drittheil des Bogens, indem man die Achtel mit geworfenen markirten Spiccato-Strichen, die Sechzehntheilgruppen mit weichern Spiccato-Strichen spielt.

Etüde 41.

REMARKS.

In regard to *Etude* 25, Adagio sostenuto, (see also preface) I would remark that the delicate placing of the bow at the frog, the slow drawing of the same, together with the swelling of the tone (without allowing the bow stick to tremble) appears to many, and rightly so, to be a very difficult operation; it should therefore be practised with great patience and accuracy. Through these studies, which are specially designed to develop essential forms of technic, additional power will be gained in the use of the upper third of the bow. Beginners generally produce much more tone at the frog (in consequence of the weight of the hand) when approaching the bridge, than at the point of the bow. This evil will be greatly overcome through a careful practise of these studies. (see also supplementary scale-studies.) Furthermore, Etude 25 affords opportunity to study the *long* trills. How necessary a finished execution of the foregoing is, the examples which the standard classical Violin-Concertos of Beethoven present, will attest. The long trills in this Etude, it will be perceived, are to be studied with the third, as well as with the fourth finger. Besides pureness of intonation in the intervals, and correctness of time, in executing long trills, one should always maintain a perfectly *smooth, steady movement of the bow,* and *a fine tone.* For *Etude* 1. What was said in the preface concerning fingerings and their effect in musical performance, the following examples will be found to substantiate. In the original edition of the Kreutzer Etudes as well as in others subsequently published, it will be perceived that the long-change occurs in No. 1., first in the 15th measure. In the present edition it is already introduced in the 9th measure and is continued to the 15th measure. This is done for the following reasons: Were the Etude to be studied in simple up and down bow-strokes, the entry introduction of the long-change would only be admissible at the 15th measure. But in attempting to execute slurred bowing, for instance, the 2d and 5th, without the long-change as in the 9th measure, I have always heard the rhythmic order of the notes as follows, while the bow must jump over the A string which lies between.

ANMERKUNGEN.

Zu *Etude* 25 Adagio sostenuto (s. auch Vorwort) möchte i noch bemerken, dass das zarte Ansetzen des Bogens am Frosch und das langsame Ziehen und Anschwellen-Lassen des Tones (oh die Stange zittern zu lassen) Vielen recht schwer fällt und daher m Ausdauer und grosser Accuratesse geübt werden muss. Durc dieses Studium wird zugleich viel Kraft am obern Drittheil d Bogens erlangt. Gewöhnlich haben besonders Anfänger am Frosc viel mehr Ton als an der Spitze (aus dem Gewichte der Ha hervorgehend,) wenn sich dieselbe dem Stege nähert) Diesem Ueb wird durch erwähntes Studium abgeholfen werden (s. auch Scale beilage).—Ferner giebt Etude 25 auch Gelegenheit, den *lang* Triller zu studiren.—Wie nöthig dessen schöne Ausführung bei Vortrage unserer Meisterwerke ist, zeigt beispielsweise das höchsten stehende classische Violinconcert, das Beethoven'sch Die langen Triller in dieser Etude sind sowohl—wie ver merkt—m dem dritten als auch mit dem vierten Finger zu studiren. Nebe der Reinheit der Intervalle und der Gleichmässigkeit der Schla achte man beim langen Triller auch darauf, dass der Bogen *imm gleichmässig fortläuft und der Ton schön bleibt.*—Zu *Etude* 1. W im Vorworte über den Fingersatz und dessen Wirkung auf d musikalischen Vortrag gesagt wurde, möchte nachfolgend durc Beispiele seine Bestätigung finden. Sowohl in der Original-Au gabe der Kreutzer'schen Etuden als auch in sämmtlichen Bearbe ungen, welche seit derselben erschienen sind, wird man in No. 1 d Lagenwechsel erst vom 15 Tact an vermerkt finden. In vorliegen Ausgabe tritt derselbe schon im 9 Tact ein, und findet bis zum 1 Tact etc. statt; dieses geschieht aus folgenden Gründen: Wäre d Etude nur im einfachen Herunter-und Heraufstrich zu studiren, wäre der Eintritt des Lagenverkehrs erst vom 15. Tact an gerech fertigt. Versucht man aber, gebundene Stricharten z. B. die zwei und fünfte, ohne Lagenwechsel vom 9. Tact ab zu executiren, habe ich die rhythmische Anordnung der Noten stets folgende massen gehört, weil die dazwischen liegende A-Saite mit dem Boge über sprungen werden muss.

better to fall thus: / in bessern Falle so:

further also with the A string sounding through
ferner auch mit durchklinger A-Saite

A better impression is made, and a more perfect quality attained by employing the fingerings indicated in the present edition, in the 9th, 10th and following measures.

Einen bessern Eindruck und zwar den vollstandiger Gleichmassigkeit macht die in vorliegender Ausgabe angewendete Applicatur im 9. 10 und den folgenden Tacten.

Etude 2, Measures 9 and 10
Etude 2, Tact 9 und 10

Concerning the numerous exercises of indicated bowings in Etude 1, I would remark that the student would do well, to acquire little by little a comprehensive knowledge of all of them, because he will meet them in their various forms in his playing later on. It is very strongly to be recommended in the case of Etudes 1, 2, 5, 8, that the student carefully consider the varied subjects presented, with their manifold bowings, that they be daily reviewed with earnest practise. They are an invaluable treasure to the violinist, for through an indefatigable and intelligent study of the same the bowing becomes more correct, finer and more elegant, while the tone of the player acquires beauty, largeness and nobleness. By this means the student will also experience the fact that in his bow-execution, through a frequent practise of the prescribed bowings, he will be enabled from day to day, in the Etude 25—long bowings with the swelling and diminishing of the tone—to play with more elegance and ease. A complete mastery of the bow technic is therefore the principal requisite for the production of an ideal tone through which musical inspirations may receive elevated rendition and be freed from all material incongruities. Without this mastery of the bow it would be impossible for the violinist to produce upon the instrument a singing and soulful expression in his renderings. (see p. 44). In pursuance of these remarks the student is recommended to make a particular selection of bowing for each day's practise, (not to go through with all of them in any particular Etude) and furthermore is earnestly reminded, however ambitious he may be to progress, not to neglect them should he meanwhile practise other technical

Bezuglich der in so reicher Anzahl bei Etude 1 verzeichneten Stricharten bemerke ich noch, dass die Studirenden sehr wohl daran thun werden, sich in sammtlichen derselben nach und nach eine bedeutende Gewandtheit anzueignen, denn sie alle werden den Geigern in der Praxis begegnen. Es ist sehr zu empfehlen, auf die Etuden 1, 2, 5, 8 mit ihren mannichfachen Stricharten taglich zuruckzukommen. Sie sind ein wahrer Schatz fur den Violinisten, da die Bogenfuhrung durch deren gewissenhaftes Studium immer correcter, gewandter, feiner und eleganter wird, und der Ton des Geigers an Gleichmassigkeit, Schonheit, Grosse und Noblesse gewinnt. Daher wird der Studirende auch die Erfahrung machen, dass seine Bogenfuhrung durch das haufige Ueben der vermerkten Stricharten einen Schliff erhalt, der ihm die Ausfuhrung der in Etude, 25 angewandten langathmigen Bogenfuhrung mit ihrem An- und Abschwellen von Tag zu Tag leichter und schoner gelingen lasst. Eine *vollstandige* Beherrschung der Bogentechnik ist daher das Haupterforderniss, den idealen Klang eines vorzutragenden musikalischen Gedankens zu erhoben und ihn von allen materiellen Schlacken zu befreien. Ohne diese Beherrschung des Bogens wird es dem Violinisten auch nicht moglich, wirklich auf der Geige zu singen und einen schonen seelenvollen Ausdruck in seine Vortrage zu legen (s. p. 44) Nach diesen Vorbemerkungen wird den Studirenden empfohlen, sich fur jeden Tag ein bestimmtes Pensum von Stricharten vorzulegen (also nicht alle auf einmal bei der betreffenden Etude durchzuarbeiten) und ferner solche, auch wenn er bei anderm technischen Material verweilt, nicht zu vernachlassigen,

materials. It is also worthy of recommendation, ultimately, before studying concert and other solo compositions, first to make preparation by practising a few exercises in bowing and finally, as well, to study effects in forte and piano. As one player shows a special talent for this, and another for that particular manner of bowing, whereby the full effect of the execution is made to appear, and still another finds it difficult to familiarize himself with some peculiar kind of bowing the following suggestions are given, which if practically taken advantage of will prove of inestimable value.

The so-called Paganini bowing, one will do well to write out entirely, or at least indicate the down-stroke (or the previous up-stroke) after every third or sixth group of sixteenth-notes, because experience has shown that in this bowing it is very easy to go amiss. The *Viotti bowing* will also seem difficult to many, but one can obtain a parallel effect by first practising the same on the open strings with a *long* bow-stroke, thereby sounding (tossing out) the second note quite energetically, and then producing the rest by suddenly stopping the movement of the bow. After thus acquiring this manner of bowing with a long stroke, one can gradually shorten it, until it is so nearly mastered that it can be executed with any degree of rapidity.

(auch ist es empfehlenswerth, spaterhin vor dem Studium Concerten und andern Solostucken seinen Bogen zuerst durch ein Stricharten vorzubereiten und letztere sowohl forte als piano studiren. Da einzelne Geiger fur diese, andere fur jene Strich besondere Begabung bezuglich deren effectvoller Ausfuhrung zeig andere wieder mit einzelnen Manieren der Bogentechnik sich ni recht befreunden konnen, mogen hier einige Winke folgen.

Die sogenannte *Paganini'sche Strichart* thut man wohl, ganz auszuschreiben, oder wenigstens hinter jeder dritten o sechsten Sechzehntheilgruppe den Herunterstrich (oder vorheri Heraufstrich) zu markiren, da die Erfahrung gezeigt hat, dass dieser Strichart sehr leicht etwas misslingt. Dann fallt die *V ti'sche Strichart* Vielen recht schwer, was man dadurch parallisi kann, dass man dieselbe zuerst auf den blanken Saiten mit *lan* Bogenstrichen ubt, dabei die zweite Note recht energisch hera tosst und hinter derselben eine Pause durch plotzliches Anhalten Bogens eintreten lasst. Kann man diese Strichart mit langen Strich in dieser Weise ausfuhren, so verkurze man dieselben bis man die Manier allmalig soweit Herr wird, sie in jeder Geschwindigkeit executiren.

Another form of bowing, with the tie, which appears difficult to many, is the staccato. In Etude 3 is a variation from the original and other editions, which consists in the staccato being indicated with a down-bow stroke. Many players think that they have the ability to produce the staccato only with the up-stroke; others (the minority) only with the down-stroke. The staccato is at once the boldest and most brilliant kind of bowing on the violin, and rightly employed, so charming an ornament to solo-playing, that one should not commit himself exclusively to the one or the other form without having made a profound study of the staccato in the down-stroke as well as in the up-stroke of the bow. Practise the staccato with the up-stroke as well as with the down-stroke, first on the open strings as exemplified in Etude 3, and then on the single tones of the scale, giving to each note two, four, six, eight or more pushes of the bow. Then play the scale ascending and descending enunciating each tone only once. Finally one should practise the staccato in broken chords, the same as presented in the Etude, besides the scales. Evenness of the notes, lightness, and the highest degree of precision in the general manner of executing this form of bowing, especially in the rhythm, are the essentials for a fine staccato.

Eine fernere fur Viele mit Schwierigkeiten verbundene Strich ist das Staccato. In Etude 3 ist abweichend von der Original-u andern Ausgaben das Staccato auch oft im Herunterstrich verzei net. Viele Geiger glauben, sie seien nur fur das Staccato Heraufstrich begabt, andere (die Minderzahl) nur fur das Stacca im Herunterstrich. Das Staccato ist aber die glanzendste u kuhnste Strichart auf der Violine und, an richtiger Stelle angebrac eine so reizende Zierde des Solospiels, dass man gut thut, sich ni zu fruh zu der einen oder der andern Meinung zu bekennen, oh die grundlichsten Studien sowohl fur das Staccato im Herunter auch im Heraufstrich gemacht zu haben. Man ube das Stacca sowohl mit dem Herauf-als auch mit dem Herunterstrich zuerst a blanken Saiten auf der bei Etude 3 besprochenen Weise, alsdann den einzelnen Tonen der Scalen, jedem Tone zwei, vier, sechs, a und mehrere Stosse gebend. Alsdann die Scalen herauf und hero terspielend, jeden Ton nur einmal angebend. Schliesslich ube m das Staccato auch in gebrochenen Accorden, wie es neben Scal auch die betreffende Etude bringt. Gleichheit der Noten, Leicht keit und hochste Genauigkeit im Rhythmus sind die Beiungung eines schonen Staccato.

SUPPLEMENT ON STACCATO ILLUSTRATION
BEILAGE ZUR STACCATO-ERLÄUTERUNG.

1) Up-bowstroke very slowly. / *Heraufstrich sehr langsam.*
2) Up-bowstroke somewhat quicker. / *Heraufstrich etwas schneller.*

It is further to be remarked that one will certainly do very well when *first* studying the staccato, to produce the tones in a single stroke with as energetic, forceful pushes of the bow as possible, and to be careful, *after acquiring dexterity* in this kind of bowing, even if a number of notes are played staccato in one stroke, to use only *the upper half of the bow.* Practise has proven that a faulty staccato execution on the up-stroke can soon be corrected through a study of the staccato with the down-stroke. The trouble thus taken to remedy this defect, cannot be considered a waste of time, as it is often called. In individual cases where it has been demonstrated, that in spite of the most careful, intelligent and well-directed study coupled with diligent practise, a good staccato with the down-stroke cannot be successfully acquired, then employ only the contrary bowing; the staccato with the up-stroke. It is advantageous in the up-stroke staccato, exceptionally, to turn the bow-hair from you, and in a manner play with the edge of the same. In practising the down-stroke staccato, it is better to use the *left* edge of the bow-hair, (turned out from the wrist) also to incline the bow-stick towards the player. Practise in this manner until success is attained. After that one will be able to do so with the full width of the bow-hair (this is necessary to a good down-stroke staccato) without difficulty in the execution of the down-stroke. (See supplementary notes). Another mode of bowing that many players do not execute correctly, is the hopping-staccato with the springing-bow, the application of which may be found in Etudes 1, 2, 5, 8, 14. It is better to practise this manner of bow-technic first on the open strings in slow notes, and in order that one may possess the utmost freedom of execution, to practice it with the up-stroke as well as the down-stroke.

Es sei hierbei noch bemerkt, dass man zwar sehr gut daran thu sich beim *ersten* Studium des Staccato moglichst ausgreifend martellirender Stosse auf einen Strich zu bedienen, dass man ab *nach erlangter Geschicklichkeit* dieses Bogenstriches darauf halte muss, auch bei vielen auf einen Strich zu staccatirenden Noten n *die obere Bogenhälfte* zu verbrauchen. Die Praxis hat ubrige gelehrt, dass eine mangelhafte Staccato-Geschicklichkeit fur d Heraufstrich durch das Studium des Herunterstrich-Staccato b verbessert wird. Die darauf verwandte Muhe ist demnach als kei Zeitvergeudung zu betrachten, was oft geschieht. Fur diejenig Falle aber, welche zeigen, dass einzelnen Individuen ein gut Staccato im Herunterstrich trotz fleissigen Uebens nicht geling will, moge die entgegensetzte Bogenhaltung des Staccato im Herau strich angewandt werden. Beim Heraufstrich-Staccato ist vortheilhaft, die Haare ausnahmsweise von sich abzuwenden u gewissermassen mit der Schneide derselben zu spielen. Beim Ueb des Herunterstrich-Staccato aber fahrt man besser, die *linke* Schn de der Haare (vom Handgelenk aus gerechnet, also die Stange na dem Spieler zugewendet) zu benutzen. Auf diese Weise ube m es bis zum Erfolg. Alsdann wird man es auch mit der ganz Breite der Haare (denn diese ist zu einem guten Herunterstric Staccato erforderlich) ohne Schwerfalligkeit im Herunterstric ausfuhren konnen. (s. Notenbeilage.)—Eine andere Strichart, b welcher sich auch viele Geiger nicht recht zu benehmen wissen, das hupfende Staccato der Springbogen, welcher bei den Eruden 2, 5, 8, 14 auch seine Verwendung findet. Auch diese Manier d Bogentechnik ubt man zuerst am besten auf blanken Saiten langsamen Noten und zwar sowohl im Herauf-als im Herunterstric

Practise the following example also on the other three strings.　　　　Vorstehende Beispiele ube man auch auf den andern 3 Saite

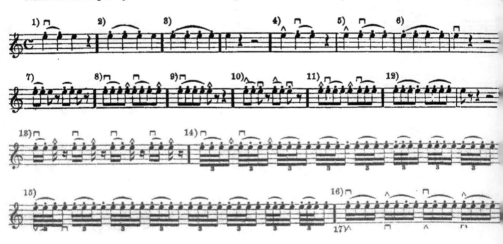

It is advantageous, however, *not to place the little finger too ~~firm~~ly upon the bow-stick, but to separate and raise it some.* By ~~ho~~lding the bow in this way the bow-stick will rebound much better ~~an~~d a full control of it will be gradually and surely acquired. ~~O~~ne will also be more able, in the springing-bow, to regulate the ~~for~~ce of the up-throwing, whether there be two, three, four or more ~~sta~~ccato notes to be played in this manner.

A special effect produced with the springing-bow is the *Arpeggio*, ~~on~~e of the most attractive features in solo playing and which is exe~~cu~~ted over two, three and four strings; also the so-called tremolo. The ~~lat~~ter consists of a continuous use of arpeggio by which the down-~~str~~oke and the immediately following up-stroke with the springing-~~bo~~w, runs over two, three or four strings. To obtain a fine execution ~~of t~~his springing-bow arpeggio, it is very necessary, during such ~~pa~~ssages, to maintain an absolute evenness of the down and up-~~str~~okes. To overcome this difficulty, take up previous studies again ~~in~~ slow notes and proceed in the following manner:—Use the middle ~~of~~ the bow 1) in moderate time, quarter notes, on the open strings, ~~an~~d to ensure the greatest precision, employ the metronome. Then ~~go~~ on to an Allegro movement 2) with these quarter notes (always ~~pla~~ying to the beat of the metronome)—then 3) with eighth notes in ~~th~~e same tempo. However, the changing on the strings must be ~~do~~ne with a sudden, lively push, without the slightest pause between ~~the~~ notes. Then proceed 4) to sixteenth-notes in Moderato Tempo, ~~th~~en 5) to sixteenth-notes in Allegretto Tempo, then 6) to sixteenth-~~no~~tes in Allegro Tempo, further 7) *to the two slurred sixteenth-notes* ~~in~~ Allegro Tempo. Having arrived at this stage of bowing, give ~~th~~e bow-stick more swing (of course being careful that the bow-hair ~~ha~~s been properly rosined, and has also been drawn up to the right ~~te~~nsion) by using a little more of the hair space, and by raising from ~~th~~e bow-stick the little and the third fingers, leaving the bow to its ~~ow~~n motions by holding it only with the thumb, index and middle ~~fin~~gers, thus producing (8) the springing motion over two strings. ~~W~~hen one has acquired this kind of bowing on two strings, he can ~~suc~~cessfully employ it upon three and four strings.

Es ist jedoch vortheilhaft, *den kleinen Finger nicht fest auf die Stange zu legen, sonder denselben etwas zu luften.* In dieser Bogenhaltung prallt die Stange viel besser zuruck. Auch richtet man beim Springbogen *die Kraft des Aufwerfens* sehr darnach ein, ob zwei, drei, vier oder mehrere Noten in dieser Weise staccatirt werden sollen.

Eine besonders effectvolle Art des Springbogen ist das *Arpeggio* im Springbogen uber zwei, drei und vier Saiten und das sogenannte Tremolo. Das Tremolo besteht in einer fortlaufender Anwendung von Arpeggien, bei welchen der Herunter-und gleich darauf zuruck der Aufstrich im Springbogen uber zwei, drei oder vier Saiten lauft. Zur schonen Ausfuhrung dieser Springbogen-Arpeggien bedarf man aber wahrend der Dauer derartiger Passagen der correctesten Gleichmassigkeit des Ab-und Aufstriches. Um diese Schwierigkeit zu uberwinden, fange man wieder mit Vorstudien in langsamen Noten und zwar in folgender Weise an: Man streiche in der Mitte des Bogens 1) im Moderato-Tempo Viertel auf den blanken Saiten an, und zwar studire man, um die grosste Genauigkeit zu erzielen, nach dem Metronom. Alsdann gehe man mit diesen Vierteln 2) in ein Allegro-Tempo uber (immer nach dem Metronom spielend) alsdann 3) zu Achtelnoten in demselben Tempo. Jedoch geschehe der Saitenwechsel jedes Mal mit einem plotzlichen lebhaften Stoss, ohne die gringste Pause zwischen den Noten. Alsdann gehe man 4) zu *Sechszehntheilen* im Moderato-Tempo uber, dann 5) zu Sechszehntheilen im Allegretto-Tempo, dann 6) zu Sechzehntheilen im Allegro-Tempo, ferner 7) *zu je zwei gebundenen Sechzehntheilen* im Allegro-Tempo. Ist man bei dieser Bogenbewegung angelangt, so giebt man der Bogenstange (naturlich darf diese die nothige Spannkraft und den wohl mit Colophonium eingeriebenen Haaren eine richtige Anspannung nicht fehlen) mehr Schwung, indem man einen etwas langeren Raum der Haare verbraucht, hebt dabei den kleinen und den Ringfinger von der Stange auf, uberlasst den Bogen seiner eigenen Bewegung, indem man ihn nur mit Daumen, Zeigefinger und Mittelfinger halt und so ist 8) die springende Bewegung uber zwei Saiten hergestellt. Kann man diese Strichart uber zwei Saiten ausfuhren, so gelingt deren Anwendung auch uber drei und vier Saiten.

When one has perfectly mastered the 8) indicated modes of ~~b~~ow-technic be may then practise the same on other strings and with ~~st~~ops

Hat man die bei 8) verzeichnete Manier der Bogentechnik gut in der angegebenen Weise erlernt und in seiner Gewalt, so ube man dieselbe auf andern Saiten und in Griffen.

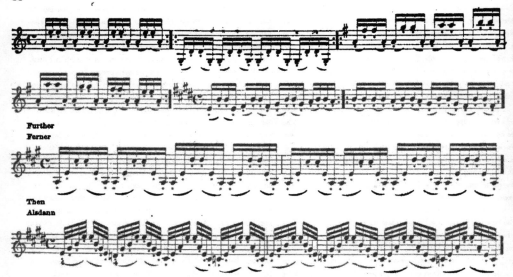

Further
Ferner

Then
Alsdann

One has only to be careful now that the bow always remains in swinging motion. This is effected by keeping the feeling in your hand and arm that *the bow is moving on its own balance*. Should the player in such, Arpeggio-study, lose the balance—which is generally the result of too long an up-stroke—it may be regained, sometimes, when thus lost, by dropping the little finger on the bow-stick, (but only at the moment of regaining the balance) when it will act as a sort of regulator. When the tremolo is to be played *continuously and evenly* on two strings, (also in double stops) it will be found very advantageous for the student to practise it first in the following manner:

Nun hat man nur noch darauf zu achten, dass der Bogen immer in Schwung bleibe. Dieses wird dadurch erreicht, dass man immer das Gefühl in der Hand und im Arme behält, *der Bogen bewege sich in seinem Schwerpunct*. Kommt der Geiger beiderartigen Arpeggien-Studien—und gewöhnlich geschieht dieses durch zu lange Heraufstriche—zuweilen vom Schwerpunct fort, so lasse er den kleinen Finger auf die Stange sinken (aber nur für den Moment des Ausgleichens, gewissermassen als Regulator), und die richtige Balance des Bogens ist wieder hergestellt. Soll der Tremolostrich aber *stets zwei Saiten zugleich* (also im Doppelgriff) fassen, so thut man gut, ihn zuerst in folgender Weise zu üben:

Finally
Schliesslich

Although the springing-bow arpeggios were not formerly reckoned among the classical forms of bow-technic, nevertheless I deem it advisable to recommend their practise (see variations in Etude 14) and to bring them more into use by a comprehensive explanation of

Obwohl man die Springbogen-Arpeggien früher nicht zu den eigentlich klassischen Manieren der Bogentechnik rechnete, hielt ich dennoch deren Anwendung (s. Varianten zu Etude 14) und deren nähere Beschreibung in dieser Ausgabe für gerathen, da sie in

em in this edition, for the reason that of late they have often been ployed in classical violin concertos. As an example I will cite the endelssohn Violin Concerto, in the first part of which the arpeggios, with a springing-bow, are immensely effective, whilst the orchestral accompaniment to the principal part of the splendid Introductory Tutti, previously heard, corroborates my views in this matter.

neuerer Zeit auch öfters im klassischen Violinconcert, angewendet worden sind. Unter andern moge das Mendelssohn'sche Violinconcert, worin Springbogen-Arpeggien im ersten Satze in höchst wirkungsvoller Weise eintreten, wahrend die Orchester-Begleitung das vorher im Verein mit der Principalstimme ausgefuhrte herrliche Einleitungs-Tutti erklingen lässt, fur meine Ansicht sprechen.

Just here I will mention the fact that many players are deficient the staccato and the springing-bow as well as in the execution of the ill, because they have become resigned to the idea that they can ver execute these technical movements with brilliancy. Practise, deed, has demonstrated that many players, despite the fact that ey have devoted zealous study to these technicalities, have nevereless been unable to successfully overcome the difficulties thereof, hilst others, less talented and with much less labored application aster them easily. As it is a matter of fact that a lack of elasticity the fingers and in the wrist can be remedied, and that experience s shown that through this means the violinist's execution can be proved, and, that in many of the above cases of resigned misprehension, it was more the want of *bodily knowing*, than the lack talent, I therefore feel duty bound to recommend a remedy at ce useful and practical, by the help of which better results may be tained and the above as well as other technical difficulties be more eedily overcome. It consists in the cultivation of the *finger, arm d wrist-joint* gymnastics. The two best books upon this subject e the "Finger and Wrist Gymnastics by Jackson," also "Gymnass of the Hand" by Ernst (both published in Leipzig.) The last amed, in particular, furnishes abundant practical and useful information. It is only from a great want of appreciation of the aportance of this means of improvement in the matter of violin chnic that it is so ignored. With common sense and moderation, the plication of the principles given in the above named books and ccompanying exercises, will develop an *extraordinary* degree of rength, flexibility and dexterity in the fingers, as well as volubility the wrists and arms, and what is more, *endurance* in playing. ut it is recommended—that these gymnastic exercises should *never* gone through with *directly before studying on the instrument*, and ove all things, as before intimated, they should never be carried to ccess. It is self-evident that the principal effort of the player ould be directed to *the attainment of a good technic*; the study of s instrument itself; nevertheless, the method of gymnastics that as been mentioned *as a valuable adjunct* in the general design particularly in certain cases—should not be allowed to escape the tention.

An dieser Stelle moge noch erwahnt werden, dass sich viele Geiger bei mangelhafter Geschicklichkeit fur die staccatirten und Springbogen—Stricharten ebenso wie bei einem mangelhaften Triller der Resignation uberlassen und sich einbilden, sie wurden es uberhaupt nie zu brillanter Ausfuhrung dieser technischen Manieren bringen. Die Praxis hat allerdings bewiesen, dass viele Geiger trotz eifrigster Studien diese Schwierigkeit nicht uberwinden konnen, dass Andere hingegen, welche im Ganzen viel weniger talentirt waren, solche ohne besonders muhsame Studien sich aneigneten.—Da sich jedoch thatsachlich herausgestellt hat, dass sich in vielen Fallen der Mangel an Elasticitat in den Fingern und im Handgelenk wirklich verbessern lasst, und die Praxis bewiesen hat, dass sich hierdurch zugleich die Geigerleistungen heben—da es sich in vielen der gedachten Fallen mehr um einen Mangel *an korperlichem Konnen* als um einen Mangel an Begabung handelt, so halte ich mich fur verpflichtet, ein nutzliches und practisches Hulfsmittel zur *schnelleren* Herbeifuhrung eines guten Resultates bei genannten und andern technischen Schwierigkeiten auszufuhren und zu empfehlen. Es besteht in der Cultivirung der *Finger-Arm-und Handgelenkgymnastik*. Die beiden besten Buchelchen hierfur sind die "Finger und Hangelenk-Gymnastik von Jackson," sowie "Gymnastik der Hand von Ernst" (beide in Leipzig erschienen). Namentlich das letztere verschafft reichen practischen Nutzen und Belehrung.—Es ist nur einem grossen Mangel an Einsicht zuzuschreiben, dass dieses so wichtige Hulfsmittel, die Violintechnik zu heben, so ignorirt wird. Mit Vernunft und Massigung angewendet, tragen die in den genannten Schriften angefuhrten Uebungen *ausserordentlich* zur Kraftigung, Biegsamkeit und Fertigkeit der Finger bei, sowie auch die Volubilitat des Handgelenks und des Arms, ferner *die Ausdauer* beim Geigen durch sie gehoben wird. Nur ist zu empfehlen, diese gymnastischen Uebungen *nie direct vor dem Studium des Instrumentes* vorzunehmen und solche vor allen Dingen, wie schon angedeutet wurde, nicht zu ubertreiben. Selbstverstandlich ist die Hauptubung des Geigers, *um gute technische Fortschritte zu erzielen*, das Studium seines Instrumentes selbst, jedoch ist die erwahnte Art der Gymnastik *als Mittel zum Zweck*—ganz besonders in gewissen Fallen—nicht ausser Acht zu lassen.

Further Fingering to Etude 5.   Weitere Applicaturen zu Etude 5.

Further: exclusively on the E string.   Ferner: ausschliesslich auf der E-Saite.

Further: on the E string as a study for the extension of the fourth finger.   Ferner: auf der E-Saite als Studie zur Ausdehnung des vierten Fingers.

Downward passage of this Etude employing the *fourth* position.   Abwärts steigende Passage dieser Etude mit Benutzung der vierten Lage.

I take occasion to remark concerning the downward passage by intervals of thirds, that in the great violin work by Baillot, "The Art of Violin-playing," in the scales of broken thirds, will be found the following fingering which in descending is not to be ignored in practise, especially when the down going intervals of thirds begin with the higher note. (The world-famous highly excellent work, "The Art of Violin-playing," which was dedicated to his scholars by that eminent artist and master of the violin, P. Baillot. (Schott Mainz.)

Bei Gelegenheit der abwärts steigenden Terzen-Intervalle möchte ich bemerken, dass man in Baillot's grossem Violin-werk "Die Kunst des Violinspiels" bei den in getrennten Terzen sich abwickelnden Scalen folgenden Fingersatz beim Heruntersteigen angewendet findet, und ist derselbe nicht in der Praxis zu ignoriren, wenn nämlich die abwärts steigenden Terzen-Intervalle mit dem hohern Ton beginnen. (Das weltberühmte höchst vorzügliche Werk, "Die Kunst des Violinspiels" seinen Schulern gewidmet von P. Baillot. (Schott, Mainz.)

Example of this from BEETHOVEN'S KREUTZER-SONATE, Op. 47 1 Form.
Beispiel hierzu aus BEETHOVEN'S KREUTZER-SONATE, Op. 47, 1 Satz:

Not so good as the fingering indicated above. The *upper* fingering is preferable to the lower because of its winged movement, and ...ause the legato passages can be rendered smoother and even...reby; one can also remain more on one and the same string than ...using the lower fingering. But then this fingering is only a real ...antage when one employs it often and in all the different ...cending scales of consecutive thirds in this form. Otherwise the ...cution thereof easily becomes insecure. In the above mentioned ...rk of Baillot, as well as in the 3d Part of Ch. de Beriot's Violin ...ool (treating of style, and appearing in the same edition) the ...dent will find numerous examples from celebrated violin studies, ...certos and chamber music works by Beriot, besides many other ...tions, belonging to dramatic vocal works, which, with the solid ...lanations that are given, furnished a rich source that taken ...antage of will endow him with a refined power of expression and ...ity of execution. Both works will contribute to bestow upon the ...nt of the violinist a higher degree of excellence.

In reference to the remarks made hereon in the Preface (see III.) ...ould recommend that the Kreutzer Trill-studies be practised daily, ...they are so very often found in concert pieces. Without a round ...d brilliant execution one will never be able, for example, to arrive ...an unexceptionally fine rendition of so grand a work as one of ...hr's violin concertos.

The succeeding parallel passages from Spohr's "Gesangsscene," ...example, show that the Kreutzer Trill-Studies can be applied to ...rantage in the same.

Weniger gut als der oben vermerkte Fingersatz. Der *obere* Fingersatz ist des geflügelten Tempo wegen dem *untern vorzuziehen*, da die Legato-Passage dadurch glatter und gleichmässiger wird, und man auch mehr auf einer und derselben Saite bleibt als beim untern Fingersatz. Eine wirkliche Erleichterung ist dieser Fingersatz aber nur dann, wenn man viel und in allen Tonarten abwärts steigende Terzen-Scalen mit demselben studirt hat. Andernfalls wurden leicht Unsicherheiten vorkommen.—In dem oben erwahnten Werke von Baillot sowie im III. Theile der Violinschule von Ch. de Beriot ("vom Styl" handelnd, erschienen in demselben Verlage) findet der Studirende auch in überaus zahlreichen Beispielen aus berühmten Violin-Etuden, Concerten, Kammermusik-Werken—bei Beriot auch ausserdem noch durch viele dem dramatischen Gesange angehörende Citate und durch höchst gediegene Auseinandersetzungen eine reichte Quelle, seine Ausdrucksfähigkeit und reinen Vortrag zu veredlen. —Beide Werke werden dazu beitragen, dem Talente der Violinisten eine höhere Weihe zu verleihen.

Hinweisend auf die hierauf bezügliche Bemerkung des Vorwortes (S. III.) empfehle ich bezüglich der Kreutzerschen Triller-Stadien täglich zu üben, da selbige so sehr oft in Concertstücken Anwendung finden. Ohne deren runde und brillante Ausführung wird man beispielsweise nicht dazu gelangen, ein Spohr'sches Concert schon vorzutragen.

Vorstehende Parallelstellen aus Spohr's Gesangsscene z. B zeigen, dass die Kreutzer'schen Trillerstudien nutzlich in derselben zu verwerthen sind.

It may well be conceded that there is scarcely a composition for the violin, even among the violin concertos of Beethoven, Mendelssohn and Max Bruch, in which the capability of the instrument to emulate the human voice is so beautifully and acceptably demonstrated as in the above mentioned Spohr "Gesangsscene." Not many players are so gifted as to be nightingales on the violin; to sing beautifully and meltingly on this first of instruments. But for those who are, and in whom there lies the possibility of higher development, the following important advice as regards the study of tone and its enoblement, may be given. Without a really beautiful, noble, sympathetic tone, a brilliant technic is but cold, however highly cultivated.—About the frequent return to a study of Etudes 1, 2, 5, 8, 14, 25, for the cultivation of the bowing, enough has already been said. A study of the following scale studies, will take one to a still higher ideal beauty of tone. *One must not be afraid of the pains to be taken, for they will surely bring their reward!*

The following scales are to be practised in the regular position and in the position, as well, indicated by the fingering marked below, with the prescribed tone-*contrasts* and tone-*shadings*, and are to be frequently gone through, with precise and careful study. Also in this edition, by a study of the different bowings that appear in the various Etudes, in conjunction with tone-contrast and the different nuances, one may still make himself useful. Scales, such as the preceding, and their various modifications must roll off even and fine as pearls, in the crescendo as well as in the decrescendo. The study of them leads to mastership.

(*Arrangement and manipulation of the Bow.*) The great importance of this matter occasions me here to make a few suggestions as to the practical management of the bow and also as to the proper preparation of the bow itself. First, about preparing the bow: Remove the edge of the projection on the inner side of the frog, so that it runs smoothly down on to the bow-stick. Through this means one will be able to lay the thumb *in* the frog and thereby obtain, first the advantage of a firmer, surer holding of the bow, and second, gain an additional portion of bow-length which enables one to bring the bow fully and more easily to the frog. (Beginners often go contrary to this rule.) Second, about the use of the bow: Most of the noted violin masters of older and later times teach, that in the use of the bow the full width of the bow-hair should be employed and that the bow-stick should be held quite "steep" over the strings. However, for the production of a fine mezzo-voice, a real nicely shaded tone, it is necessary to play more with the edge of the hair

Es giebt wohl mit Einschluss der Violinconcerte von Beethov Mendelssohn und Max Bruch kaum eine Composition für die Violi welche die Fähigkeit des Instrumentes, mit der menschlichen Stim zu wetteifern, in so schöner und dankbarer Weise hervortreten la wie Spohr's eben erwähnte Gesangsscene. Nicht vielen Geigern der Nachtigallenschlag auf der Geige, die Gabe, auf dem ersten Instrumente wirklich schön und schmelzend zu singen, verlieh worden. Für diejenigen aber, in welchen sie liegt und einer hohe Entwicklung fähig ist, mögen hier noch einige wichtigen Rathschla auf Ton zu studiren und ihn zu veredlen, folgen. Ohne ein wirklich schönen, edlen, sympathischen Ton lässt auch eine brilla Technik kalt, und wäre sie noch so hoch ausgebildet.—Auf häufige Zurückkehren des Studiums von Etude 1, 2, 5, 8, 14, 25, Ausbildung der Bogenführung ist genügend hingewiesen worde Zu noch höherer idealerer Schönheit des Tons wird den Studirend nachfolgendes Scalenstudium führen. *Die Mühe desselben scheue m nicht, denn sie wird ihren Lohn finden!*

Anm: Die nachfolgenden Scalen sind sowohl in fester Lage auch im Lagenverkehr mit den angegebenen Ton-*Contrasten* u. Ton-*Schattirungen* oft einem genauen und sorgfaltigem Studium unterziehen.—Auch die in dieser Ausgabe mit verschiedene Stricharten versehenen Etüden kann man sich durch das Studi mit Ton-Contrasten und verschiedenen Nuancen noch nützlic machen.—Derartige Scalen wie die vorstehenden und deren Ver rungen müssen gleichmässig und schön wie Perlen sowohl Crescendo als auch im Decrescendo herunterrollen. Das Studi derselben führt zur Meisterschaft.

(*Bogeneinrichtung u. Führung*) Die grosse Wichtigkeit d Gegenstandes veranlasst mich, hier einige Winke über die zwec mässigste Art der Bogenführung und Bogeneinrichtung zu gebe Zuerst über Bogeneinrichtung: Man entferne den eckigen Vorspru im Innern des Frosches, so dass dieser in die Stange verlauft. Dadur ist man im Stande, den Daumen *in* den Frosch zu legen, wodur man erstens den Vortheil einer festeren und sicherern Bogenhaltu erlangt, zweitens gewinnt man dadurch auch ein Stück Bogenläng indem man den Bogen leichter bis an den Frosch verbrauch (Anfänger handeln oft gegen diese Regel.) Zweitens über Boge führung: Die meisten der bedeutendsten Violinmeister älterer u neuer Zeit lehren, den Bogen mit der ganzen Breite der Haare führen und die Stange steil über den Saiten zu halten. Es ist jedo zur Hervorbringung eines schönen Mezza voce, eines recht fe nuansirten Tones nothwendig, mehr mit der Schneide der Haare

to incline the bow-stick more towards the fingerboard. The
on for this is as follows: The friction of the bow-hairs at the
it of contact with the strings is not even. For this reason the
e sounds more covered when the full width of the bow-hair is em-
ved than it does when as few hairs as possible are used; in which
e the strings are more easily made to vibrate, the tone is clearer,
nds more idealistic, and *also carries further*. The above men-
ied defect, also, does not become lost through the acoustic prop-
es or the largeness of the hall in which one plays; for a well-
ned ear will detect the same in the farthest corner of the hall
ost as well as when near the performers. In forte, crescendo,
l in certain bowings in the middle of the bow, also in chords, it is
ossible to avoid using the entire width of the bowhair. But as
usually plays with a medium degree of strength, this style of
ring is strongly recommended as well for cantilene as for ordinary
ages, and all students, especially those studying with the in-
tion of becoming soloists are urgently advised to acquire a
stery of it. Careful attention must be exercised when one is
cuting a down-bow, *piano*, *not* to bend the wrist inward as the
v is drawn towards the point; but it is quite different with the
n-bow in *forte*, in which case the bending in must occur. Pro-
sor Joachim played in this manner and also applied it to various
er kinds of steady bowing. He is very strict on this point, in
erintending the studies of his pupils of the Royal Academy of
sic, Berlin. Of our predecessors it is known, for instance, that
tti and Rode were heard to employ the above mentioned bowing.
this manner the objectionable intermingling of the tones may be
de to gradually disappear; the tone will become softer and more
apathetic, the graduation of nuances (tone-coloring) easier and
her, the effect of the whole performance enobled, and conse-
ntly a much greater impression will be made upon the cultivated
ener.

spielen und die Stange mehr dem Griffbrett zuzuneigen. Der Grund
hierfur ist folgender: Die Reibungen der Haare des Bogens sind in
ihren Beruhrungspuncten mit den Saiten nicht gleichmassig. Der
Ton klingt aus diesem Grunde beim Gebrauch der ganzen Haarbreite
gedeckter, als wenn man nur mit moglichst wenigen Haaren spielt,
wobei die Saite leichter vibrirt, der Ton klarer, idealer klingt und
auch weiter tragt. Es geht vorhin erwahnter Uebelstand auch nicht
durch die Akustik oder die Grosse des Saales, in welchem man
vortragt, verloren, denn ein geubtes Ohr bemerkt denselben in der
entferntesten Ecke des Saales fast ebenso als in der Nahe des Spielers.
Beim Forte, bei Crescendi, bei gewissen Stricharten in der Mitte des
Bog., bei Accorden lasst sich allerdings der Verbrauch der ganzen
Haarbreite nicht vermeiden. Da man aber fur gewohnlich in den
mittleren Starkegraden spielt, so ist diese anempfohlene Art der
Bogenfuhrung sowohl fur die Cantilene als auch fur Passagen sehr
empfehlenswerth und allen Studirenden, besonders denjenigen,
welche sich zu Solisten ausbilden wollen, sehr anzurathen, sich diese
Art der Bogenfuhrung zu eigen zu machen. Es wird noch darauf
aufmerksam gemacht, dass man, wenn man *in Piano* beim Herunterstrich an der Spitze angelangt ist, das Hangelenk *nicht* einknickt;
etwas Anderes ist es aber beim Herunterstrich *im Forte* da muss das
Einknicken geschehen. Professor Joachim spielt in dieser Weise
und mit der auseinandergesetzten Bogenfuhrung. Er halt auch an
der von ihm dirigirten Kgl. Hochschule der Musik zu Berlin bei
seinen Schulern consequent darauf. Von unsern Vorfahren ist bekannt,
dass namentlich Viotti und Rode mit der angegebenen Bogenfuhrung
sich horen liessen. Durch diese Manier werden die materiellen
Beimischungen des Tones immer mehr verschwinden, dieser wird
weicher und sympathischer, der Nuancenschmuck leichter und
reicher hervorgebracht werden; das ganze Spiel wird veredelt und
einen grosseren Eindruck auf den feiner organisirten Zuhorer
machen.

Scales in Different Tone-Colors and Tone-Contrasts.
Scalen in verschiedenen Klangfarben und Ton-Contrasten.

94

NB. Each of the following scales can also be studied first in whole notes with the different contrasts of tone.

NB. Jede der nachfolgenden Scalen kann man querst in ganzen Noten mit den verschiedenen Tontrasten studiren.

SCALES WITH NUANCES.
NÜANCIRTE SCALEN.

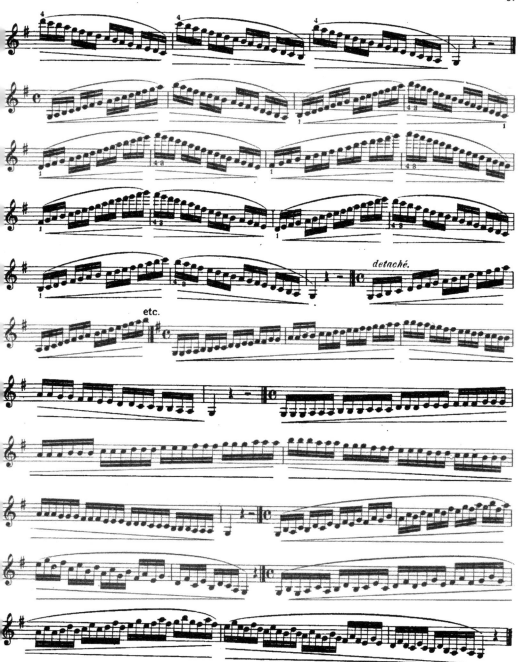

98

etc.

Finally I will mention the so-called "muted ...le" which consists in endeavoring to sustain a tone of the scale at least one minute, and softly as to be scarcely audible. Viotti imparted this specialty only to his favorite scholars, as the most precious secret of violin technique to be entrusted with. A good execution of same is truly to be called a masterpiece. In order to bring about this result, begin with 8, afterwards with 16, slow Quarter notes in one stroke of the bow, pianissimo, and on arriving at the point or frog of the bow, rest the same, every time, the duration of 8 or 16 Quarter notes, and then draw again *after* the pause. In this manner while remaining in a perfectly quiet position, in plastic pose, *and whilst touching the string with only one hair at the edge of the bow*, endeavor to move it with greatest evenness, without the least shade of trembling, for a minute or more, omitting the previously mentioned pause. The practise of the muted-scale is the best means of preparation for one who is about to make a public appearance as a soloist; and such as are liable to that excitement which is sometimes attendant upon soloplaying, it is to be recommended as an excellent means whereby one may gain necessary composure during the pauses between the solo numbers of the same evening's concert... In closing this work I would once more recommend to the student the importance of an exact appreciation of the markings of the technical matters in the same as well as of retaining the advantage of what has been given in the Remarks, so that of every violinist the fine saying of Ballot's in his great work "The Art of Violin-playing *Savoir travailler es un talent* (knowing how to work is a talent) will be confirmed.

Schliesslich erwähne ich noch des Studiums der sogenannten "stummen Tonleiter" welches darin besteht, dass man sich bestrebt, jeden Ton einer Scala wenigstens eine Minute lang kaum hörbar auszuhalten. Viotti soll dieses Verfahren nur seinen Lieblingsschülern als das kostbarste Geheimniss der Violintechnik anvertraut haben. Die gute Ausführung derselben ist auch mit Recht ein Meisterstück zu nennen. Um es dahin zu bringen, fange mit 8, später mit 16 langsamen Vierteln auf einen Strich im Pianissimo an, lasse den Bogen 8 oder 16 Viertel lang jedes Mal, wenn man an der Spitze oder am Frosch angelangt ist, still stehen, und ziehe denselben nach dieser Pause dann weiter. In dieser Weise suche man, während man in vollständig richtiger Haltung verbleibt, in plastischer Ruhe, und indem man die Saite nur mit einem Haare der Bogenschneide berührt, *es allmälig dahin zu bringen, dass der Bogen ohne jedes störende Rütteln in grösster Gleichmässigkeit* eine Minute lang und darüber sich fortbewegt, *wobei man aber die vorhin erwähnten Pausen fortlässt. Die stumme Tonleiter ist das beste Mittel, sich für das Auftreten als Solist vor dem Publicum vorzubereiten, und ist auch Solchen, welche durch Solovorträge leicht in Aufregung gerathen, als vortreffliches Mittel anzuempfehlen, sich in den auf ihre Vorträge folgenden Pausen die nöthige Fassung für die nächste an demselben Concertabend dem Publicum vorzuführende Solo-Nummer zu erringen.—Indem ich diese Arbeit schliesse, möchte ich den Studirenden noch einmal empfehlen, sich genau an die Bezeichnung des technischen Stoffes in derselben und ebenso an die in den Anmerkungen gegebenen Vortheile zu halten, damit auf jeden dieser Violinisten der schöne Ausspruch Baillot's, den er in seinem grossen Werk,* "die Kunst des Violinspiels" *gethan* "Savoir travailler est un talent *seine Bestätigung finden könne!*

FINE.   *FINE.*

Edition White-Smith

A Select Library of Standard Instruction Works, Containing Methods, Stu[dies,] Exercises and Recreations. (*Instrumental and Vocal.*) Send for Complete Cat[alogue.]

WHEN ORDERING, ALWAYS MENTION EDITION WHITE-SMITH and NUMBER

No.			Retail
1	BACH, J. S. Two- and Three-part Inventions	Piano Solo	$.60
2	BEETHOVEN, L. VAN. Sonatas, Vol. I	Piano Solo	1.50
3	BERTINI, H. Op. 29. Twenty-four Studies (*Frantz*)	Piano Solo	.40
4	BERTINI, H. Op. 32. Twenty-four Studies (*Frantz*)	Piano Solo	.40
5	BERTINI, H. Op. 29, 32. Forty-eight Studies (*Frantz*)	Piano Solo	.50
6	BERTINI, H. Op. 100. Twenty-five Easy Studies	Piano Solo	.40
7	KOHLER, L. Op. 50. Twenty Primary Studies	Piano Solo	.50
8	BURGMÜLLER, F. Op. 100. Twenty-five Easy and Progressive Studies	Piano Solo	.50
9	BURGMÜLLER, F. Op. 109. Eighteen Characteristic Studies	Piano Solo	.50
10	CHOPIN, F. Nineteen Nocturnes (*Klindworth*)	Piano Solo	.60
11	CHOPIN, F. Fourteen Waltzes (*Köhler*)	Piano Solo	.50
12	CZERNY, C. Op. 500. Grand Scale Exercises	Piano Solo	.50
13	CLEMENTI, M. Gradus ad Parnassum — 29 Selected Studies (*Tausig*)	Piano Solo	.75
14	CLEMENTI, M. Op. 36, 37, 38. Sonatines (*Köhler*)	Piano Solo	.50
15	CZERNY, C. Op. 139. One Hundred Easy Progressive Lessons (*Frantz*)	Piano Solo	.50
16	BIEHL, E. Op. 7. Easy Melodious Studies	Piano Solo	.75
17	CZERNY, C. Op. 553. Six Octave Studies	Piano Solo	.30
18	BURGMÜLLER, F. Op. 105. Twelve Brilliant and Melodious Studies	Piano Solo	.50
19	CZERNY, C. Op. 823. The Little Pianist, Book I	Piano Solo	.50
20	CZERNY, C. Op. 823. The Little Pianist, Book II	Piano Solo	.50
21	CZERNY, C. Op. 823. The Little Pianist, Complete	Piano Solo	.90
22	CZERNY, C. Op. 849. Thirty New Studies in Technics	Piano Solo	.50
23	MAZAS, F. Violin School (*Blumenstengel*)	Violin Solo	1.25
24	DIABELLI, A. Op. 125. First Twelve Lessons	Piano Solo	.25
25	DUVERNOY, J. B. Op. 120. School of Mechanism	Piano Solo	.50
26	GRIEG, E. Op. 46. Peer Gynt, Suite I	Piano Solo	.75
27	GURLITT, C. Op. 101. Album Leaves for the Young	Piano Solo	.50
28	GURLITT, C. Op. 107. Buds and Blossoms	Piano Solo	.50
29	HALLÉ, C. Piano Tutor — Section I, No. 1	Piano Solo	.75
30	HAYDN, J. Ten Celebrated Sonatas (*Winkler*)	Piano Solo	.60
31	HELLER, ST. Op. 45. Twenty-five Studies	Piano Solo	1.00
32	CZERNY, C. Op. 802. Practical Finger Exercises, Book I	Piano Solo	.50
33	CZERNY, C. Op. 802. Practical Finger Exercises, Book II	Piano Solo	.50
34	HELLER, ST. Op. 46. Thirty Progressive Studies	Piano Solo	1.00
35	MOSCHELES, I. Op. 70. Twenty-four Studies, Book I	Piano Solo	.60
36	MOSCHELES, I. Op. 70. Twenty-four Studies, Book II	Piano Solo	.60
37	HELLER, ST. Op. 47. Twenty-five Studies for Rhythm and Expression	Piano Solo	1.00
38	SPINDLER, F. Op. 44. May Bells (12 Little Songs Without Words)	Piano Solo	.50
39	BOHM, C. Op. 250a. Birthday Music	Piano (Four Hands)	1.00
40	HERZ, H. Scales and Exercises	Piano Solo	.30
41	JENSEN, A. Op. 32. Twenty-five Studies	Piano Solo	.50
42	WAGNER, E. D. Op. 45. First Piano Method, Part I (*Boards* $1.25)	Piano Solo	1.00
43	WAGNER, E. D. Op. 45. First Piano Method, Part II (*Boards* $1.25)	Piano Solo	1.00
44	KÖHLER, L. Op. 157. Twelve Little Studies	Piano Solo	.50
45	KÖHLER, L. Op. 190. Very First Studies	Piano Solo	.50
46	KÖHLER, L. Op. 210. Kinder Album	Piano Solo	.50
47	KÖHLER, L. Op. 218. Exercises and Melodies for Children	Piano Solo	.50
48	KÖHLER, L. Op. 242. Little School of Velocity	Piano Solo	.50
49	KÖHLER, L. Op. 249. Practical Piano Method, Vol. I	Piano Solo	.50
50	KÖHLER, L. Op. 249. Practical Piano Method, Vol. II	Piano Solo	.50
51	KÖHLER, L. Op. 249. Practical Piano Method, Vol. III	Piano Solo	.50
52	KÖHLER, L. Op. 249. Practical Piano Method, Vol. IV	Piano Solo	.50
53	KÖHLER, L. Op. 249. Practical Piano Method, Vol. V	Piano Solo	
54	KÖHLER, L. Op. 249. Practical Piano Method, Vol. VI	Piano Solo	
55	KÖHLER, L. Op. 300. Practical Piano Method, Vol. I	Piano Solo	
56	KÖHLER, L. Op. 300. Practical Piano Method, Vol. II	Piano Solo	
57	KÖHLER, L. Op. 300. Practical Piano Method — Complete	Piano Solo	
58	KÖHLER, L. Op. 151. Twelve Preparatory Lessons	Piano Solo	
59	KÖHLER, L. Sonatine Album	Piano Solo	
60	KUHLAU, FR. Op. 20, 55, 59. Twelve Sonatinas, Book I (*Köhler*)	Piano Solo	
61	KUHLAU, FR. Op. 20, 55, 59. Seven Sonatinas, Book II (*Roitzsch*)	Piano Solo	
62	KUHNER, C. Album of Instructive Pieces, Vol. I	Piano Solo	
63	KULLAK, TH. Op. 62, 81. Youthful Days	Piano Solo	
64	LE COUPPEY, F. Op. 17. The Alphabet	Piano Solo	
65	LE COUPPEY, F. Op. 20. L'Agilité	Piano Solo	
66	LEMOINE, H. Op. 37. Fifty Juvenile Studies	Piano Solo	
67	LOESCHHORN, A. Op. 65. Studies for Beginners, Book I	Piano Solo	
68	LOESCHHORN, A. Op. 65. Studies for Beginners, Book II	Piano Solo	
69	LOESCHHORN, A. Op. 65. Studies for Beginners, Book III	Piano Solo	
70	LOESCHHORN, A. Op. 65. Studies for Beginners — Complete	Piano Solo	
71	LOESCHHORN, A. Op. 66. Progressive Studies, Book I	Piano Solo	
72	LOESCHHORN, A. Op. 66. Progressive Studies, Book II	Piano Solo	
73	LOESCHHORN, A. Op. 66. Progressive Studies, Book III	Piano Solo	
74	LOESCHHORN, A. Op. 66. Progressive Studies — Complete	Piano Solo	
75	LOESCHHORN, A. Technical Studies	Piano Solo	
76	BERTINI, H. Method for the Pianoforte (*Boards*)	Piano Solo	
77	MENDELSSOHN, F. 49 Songs Without Words	Piano Solo	
78	MOZART, W. A. 18 Sonatas (*Winkler*)	Piano Solo	
79	OESTEN, TH. Op. 61. May Flowers (25 Little Recreations)	Piano Solo	
80	PLAIDY, L. Technical Studies	Piano Solo	
81	SCHMITT, A. 213 Five Finger Exercises	Piano Solo	
82	SCHUMANN, R. Op. 15. Scenes from Childhood	Piano Solo	
83	SCHUMANN, R. Op. 68, 15. Album for the Young and Scenes from Childhood	Piano Solo	
84	CESI, B. Method for the Piano, Part I	Piano Solo	
85	STAMATY, C. Fundamental Studies, Vol. I (*Lavallée*)	Piano Solo	
86	STAMATY, C. Fundamental Studies, Vol. II (*Lavallée*)	Piano Solo	
87	DAMM, G. Piano School. (*Boards*)	Piano Solo	
88	DIABELLI, A. Op. 149. Twenty-eight Melodious Pieces on Five Notes	Piano (Four-Hand)	
89	HUNTEN, F. Piano Method. (*Boards*)	Piano Solo	
90	LÖW, JOS. Op. 191. Tone Pictures	Piano (Four Hand[s])	
91	LÖW, JOS. Teacher and Pupil, Book I	Piano (Four Hand[s])	
92	LÖW, JOS. Teacher and Pupil, Book II	Piano (Four Hand[s])	
93	WOHLFAHRT, H. Op. 87. The Children's Friend	Piano (Four Han[ds])	
94	DANCLA, CH. Op. 52. Elementary and Progressive Method, Vol. I	Violin Solo	
95	DANCLA, CH. Op. 52. Elementary and Progressive Method, Vol. II	Violin Solo	
96	DE BERIOT, CH. Op. 102. Violin School, Part I	Violin Solo	
97	DE BERIOT, CH. Op. 102. Violin School, Part II	Violin Solo	
98	FIORILLO, F. 36 Studies or Caprices (*Bytovetzki*)	Violin Solo	
99	HENNING, CH. Op. 15. School for the Violin, Part I	Violin Solo	
100	HENNING, CH. Op. 15. School for the Violin, Part II	Violin Solo	

Edition White-Smith

Select Library of Standard Instruction Works, Containing Methods, Studies, Exercises and Recreations. (*Instrumental and Vocal.*) Send for Complete Catalog.

WHEN ORDERING, ALWAYS MENTION EDITION WHITE-SMITH and NUMBER

		Retail
...NNING, CH. Op. 15. School for the Violin, Part III	Violin Solo	$ .75
...NNING, CH. Op. 15. School for the Violin — Complete ... (*Boards*)	Violin Solo	1.50
...RMANN, F. Violin School, Book I	Violin Solo	.75
...RMANN, F. Violin School, Book II	Violin Solo	.75
...HMANN, C. H. Practical Violin School, Part I	Violin Solo	.50
...HMANN, C. H. Practical Violin School, Part II	Violin Solo	.50
...HMANN, C. H. Practical Violin School, Part III	Violin Solo	.50
...HMANN, C. H. Practical Violin School, Part IV	Violin Solo	.50
...HMANN, C. H. Practical Violin School, Part V	Violin Solo	.50
...YSER, H. E. Op. 20. 36 Études, Book I	Violin Solo	.50
...YSER, H. E. Op. 20. 36 Études, Book II	Violin Solo	.50
...YSER, H. E. Op. 20. 36 Études — Complete	Violin Solo	.75
BACH, K. Prize Piano School .. (*Boards*)	Piano Solo	2.00
...EUTZER, R. 42 Studies or Caprices (*Kross*)	Violin Solo	.50
...EUTZER, R. 42 Studies or Caprices (*Bytovetzski*)	Violin Solo	.50
...ZAS, F. Op. 36. 75 Melodious and Progressive Studies (*Schultz*)	Violin Solo	
...ZAS, F. Op. 36. Book I — 30 Special Studies	Violin Solo	.60
...ZAS, F. Op. 36. Book II — 27 Brilliant Studies	Violin Solo	.60
...ZAS, F. Op. 36. Book III — 18 Artist Studies	Violin Solo	.60
HUBERT, L. Op. 50. Violin School, Vol. I	Violin Solo	.75
HUBERT, L. Op. 50. Violin School, Vol. II	Violin Solo	.75
...RADIECK, H. Scale Studies	Violin Solo	.50
URS, B. The Violin (*Davenport*)	Violin Solo	.75
...HLFAHRT, FR. Op. 45. 258 Daily Exercises	Violin Solo	.50
...HLFAHRT, FR. Op. 45. Sixty Studies, Book I (1st Pos.)	Violin Solo	.50
...HLFAHRT, FR. Op. 45. Sixty Studies, Book II (3d Pos.)	Violin Solo	.50
...HLFAHRT, FR. Op. 74. 50 Easy and Melodious Studies, Book I (1st Pos.)	Violin Solo	.50
...HLFAHRT, FR. Op. 74. 50 Easy and Melodious Studies, Book II (3d Pos.)	Violin Solo	.50
...HLFAHRT, FR. Op. 38. Elementary Method	Violin Solo	1.00
...RADIECK, H. Chord Studies	Violin Solo	.50
...EYEL, I. Op. 48. Six Easy and Progressive Duets	Two Violins	.50
...NCLA, CH. Op. 89. Six Airs with Variations (6 *petits airs variés*)	Violin and Piano	.75
...DE, P. Concerto No. 4 (*Hermann*)	Violin and Piano	
...AMER, J. B. 50 Selected Studies, Part I (*von Bülow*)	Piano Solo	.50
...AMER, J. B. 50 Selected Studies, Part II (*von Bülow*)	Piano Solo	.50
...AMER, J. B. 50 Selected Studies, Part III (*von Bülow*)	Piano Solo	.50
...AMER, J. B. 50 Selected Studies, Part IV (*von Bülow*)	Piano Solo	.50
...AMER, J. B. 50 Selected Studies — Complete (*von Bülow*) (*Limp Cloth or Paper*)	Piano Solo	1.50
...HNKE and PEARCE. Voice Training Exercises for Soprano	Vocal	.75
...HNKE and PEARCE. Voice Training Exercises for Mezzo Soprano	Vocal	.75
...HNKE and PEARCE. Voice Training Exercises for Bass	Vocal	.75
...NA, P. Rhythmical Articulation (*English and Italian Text*)	Vocal	1.00
...NCONE, J. Op. 9. Fifty Lessons for Medium Voice, Book I (*with words*)	Vocal	.75
...NCONE, J. Op. 9. Fifty Lessons for Medium Voice, Book II (*with words*)	Vocal	.75
...NCONE, J. Op. 12. Fifteen Vocalises for Soprano or Mezzo	Vocal	.50
...NCONE, J. Op. 17. 40 Lessons for Low Voice	Vocal	.50

No.			Retail
146	LÜTGEN, B. Velocity Studies, Vol. I — Soprano	Vocal	$ .50
147	TOWER, W. C. Standard Vocal Exercises and Solfeggios for Medium Voice	Vocal	.50
148	LENZ, W. (*Arr.*) Classics for the Young	Piano Solo	.60
149	STAINER, J. The Organ	Organ	1.00
150	CZERNY, C. Op. 409. Fifty Grand Finishing Studies, Book I	Piano Solo	1.25
151	CZERNY, C. Op. 409. Fifty Grand Finishing Studies, Book II	Piano Solo	1.25
152	CZERNY, C. Op. 409. Fifty Grand Finishing Studies, Book III	Piano Solo	1.25
153	WIECK, F. Piano Studies	Piano Solo	.60
154	LEBERT and STARK. Piano School, Part I (*Boards*)	Piano Solo	1.00
155	LEBERT and STARK. Piano School, Part II (*Boards*)	Piano Solo	1.00
156	LEBERT and STARK. Piano School, Part III. (*Boards*)	Piano Solo	1.00
157	LEBERT and STARK. Piano School, Part IV (*Boards*)	Piano Solo	3.50
158	BEYER, F. Op. 101. Elementary Method (*Hearts*) ... *Boards* $1.50	Piano Solo	.75
159	FERRARA, B. The Study of the Violin, Book I	Violin Solo	1.00
160	OESTEN, TH. Op. 94. Golden Pearls	Piano Solo	.30
161	CZERNY, C. Op. 299. School of Velocity, Book I	Piano Solo	.25
162	CZERNY, C. Op. 299. School of Velocity, Book II	Piano Solo	.25
163	CZERNY, C. Op. 299. School of Velocity, Book III	Piano Solo	.25
164	CZERNY, C. Op. 299. School of Velocity, Book IV	Piano Solo	.25
165	CZERNY, C. Op. 299. School of Velocity — Complete	Piano Solo	.60
166	LOESCHHORN, A. Op. 136. School of Velocity, Book I	Piano Solo	.50
167	LOESCHHORN, A. Op. 136. School of Velocity, Book II	Piano Solo	.50
168	LOESCHHORN, A. Op. 136. School of Velocity, Book III	Piano Solo	.50
169	LOESCHHORN, A. Op. 84. Sixty Melodious Studies for Beginners, Book I	Piano Solo	.50
170	LOESCHHORN, A. Op. 84. Sixty Melodious Studies for Beginners, Book II	Piano Solo	.50
171	LOESCHHORN, A. Op. 84. Sixty Melodious Studies for Beginners, Book III	Piano Solo	.50
172	ALARD, D. Complete and Progressive Method, Book I (*Kanrich*)	Violin Solo	1.00
173	ALARD, D. Complete and Progressive Method, Book II (*Kanrich*)	Violin Solo	1.00
174	MAZAS, F. Complete Violin Method and Pleyel's Duets, Op. 8 (*Boards*)	Violin Solo	1.00
175	WICHTL, G. The Young Violinist (*Boards* $1.25)	Violin Solo	1.00
176	STREABBOG, L. Op. 63. Twelve Easy Melodious Studies	Piano Solo	.75
177	STREABBOG, L. Op. 64. Twelve Easy Melodious Studies	Piano Solo	.75
178	BRANZOLI, G. Method for the Mandolin	Mandolin	1.25
179	CHRISTOFARO, F. de. Method for the Mandolin, Vol. I	Mandolin	1.00
180	CHRISTOFARO, F. de. Method for the Mandolin, Vol. II	Mandolin	1.00
181	SMITH, W. F. Complete Method for the Mandolin	Mandolin	.50
182	CARCASSI, M. Method for the Guitar — Complete (*Jacobs*) (*Boards*)	Guitar	1.50
183	CARCASSI, M. Method for the Guitar — Abridged (*Jacobs*) (*Boards*)	Guitar	1.25
184	BERBIGUIER, B. T. Method for the Flute and L. Drouet's 21 Studies in all Keys (*Bds*)	Flute	1.25
185	KLOSÉ, H. Method for the Clarinet — Complete and Küffner's 50 Progressive Duets	Clarinet	3.00
186	KLOSÉ, H. Method for the Clarinet — Abridged and Küffner's 50 Progressive Duets	Clarinet	1.50
187	KLOSÉ, H. Fifteen Grand Morceaux	Two Clarinets	.75
188	KÜFFNER, J. Op. 80. Fifty Progressive Duets	Two Clarinets	.75
189	ARBAN, J. B. Method for the Cornet. Abridged	Cornet	1.00
190	SAINT-JACOME. Grand Method for the Cornet, Part I	Cornet	1.00
191	KUMMER, F. A. School for the Violoncello	Violoncello	1.50

CPSIA information can be obtained
at www.ICGtesting.com
Printed in the USA
LVHW081344110921
697621LV00010B/384